EXPOSING THE "CULTURE

OF ARROGANCE"

IN THE ACADEMY

A Blueprint for Increasing Black Faculty
Satisfaction in Higher Education

Gail L. Thompson
Angela C. Louque

Sty/us

STERLING, VIRGINIA

COPYRIGHT © 2005 BY
STYLUS PUBLISHING, LLC

Published by Stylus Publishing, LLC
22883 Quicksilver Drive
Sterling, Virginia 20166–2102

Library of Congress Cataloging-in-Publication Data
    Thompson, Gail L., 1957–
        Exposing the "culture of arrogance" in the
    academy : a blueprint for increasing Black faculty
    satisfaction in higher education / Gail L. Thompson
    and Angela Louque.—1st ed.
            p.   cm.
        Includes bibliographical references and index.
        ISBN 1-57922-112-2 (hardcover : alk. paper)—
        ISBN 1-57922-113-0 (pbk. : alk. paper)
        1. African American college teachers—Social
    conditions.   2. African American college teachers
    —Job satisfaction.   3. African American college
    teachers—Attitudes.   4. Educational surveys—
    United States.   5. United States—Race relations.
    I. Louque, Angela, 1960–   II. Title.
    LC2781.5.T56   2005
    378.1'2'08996073—dc22

    2004030401

ISBN: 1–57922–112–2 (CLOTH)
ISBN: 1–57922–113–0 (PAPER)

Printed in the United States of America

All first editions printed on acid-free paper
that meets the American National Standards Institute
Z39–48 Standard.

First Edition, 2005

10 9 8 7 6 5 4 3 2 1

ACKNOWLEDGMENTS

From Both of Us

WE WOULD LIKE to thank Angela Beamon, who helped to distribute questionnaires and assisted with the telephone interviews, and Martina Berry, Tyrone Johnson, and Venetta Cash for helping to distribute and collect questionnaires, as well as Dr. Ozzie Smith Jr. for his encouragement and assistance, and Dr. Randall Lindsey for his suggestions about the book. We are sending out a special thanks to John von Knorring for allowing us to add this book to the very impressive list of diversity-related books that Stylus has already published and for his commitment to diversifying the scholarly canon.

From Gail

First, I wish to thank Angela for her role in the creation of this book project. I would also like to thank my husband, Rufus, and children, Nafissa, NaChe', and Stephen for granting me time to write. As always, I am grateful to Dr. David E. Drew, who not only mentored me during my days as a doctoral student, but has provided sage advice, guidance, and unwavering support as I underwent "junior faculty boot camp" at three institutions, the tenure process, and as I continue to learn the lessons that I need to learn in order to "thrive" in the Academy, and also for his valuable feedback about this book. Dr. Agnes Moreland Jackson, Dr. Judith Jackson, and Dr. Mildred Henry, professors emeriti, have been kind, compassionate, and willing to offer advice from the vantage point of being seasoned African American professors. Some of my current colleagues, such as Dr. Lourdes Arguelles, Dr. Daryl Smith, and Dr. Jean Lipman-Blumen (an excellent role model to women and junior faculty), Associate Provost Teresa Shaw, Betty Hagelbarger, Teresa Wilborn, and Ethel Rogers, and my friends Dr. June Hetzel, Dr. Melody Lark, Dr. Camille Mayers, and Dr. Marilyn Joshua have helped me to get through many periods when I was truly frustrated with the Academy. I am also extremely grateful to President Steadman Upham (who encouraged me to keep drawing and painting) and President Ann Hart for being excellent and supportive administrators who are committed to diversifying the faculty and improving the institutional climate of postsecondary institutions. Last but not least, I am grateful to Dr. Matthew Jenkins and Roberta Jenkins for being strong supporters of faculty and students of color.

From Angela

My thankfulness goes to Gail, who has steered the development of this book. Gail has provided me with a sense of "I can-do-it-ness" and inspiration. I have valued our personal and professional friendship over the years. I'd like to thank my husband, Gene, and my children, Nicholas and Gena, for being patient and excited about this book project. I'd like to also thank my former colleagues: Dr. Carol Franklin for being an activist for social justice and a role model for mentoring young Black scholars, Dr. Karen Davidson, Dr. Helen Garcia, Dr. Cynthia Jew, Dr. Reyes Quezada, and Dr. Lily Rivera. I am also grateful to my sister-friends who have listened over the years to my stories about my journey through the Academy: Greta Bilbrew, Pamela Burnett, Tamela R. Cash-Curry, Esq., Shalita Cunningham, LaTonja Davis, Regina Drake, Barbara Douglass Gosey, Susan Haynes, Robbye Choice Howard, Beverly LeMay, Dr. Joan Roberts, Janice Ruth, Jonée Shady, Sharon Teuben-Rowe, and Lourdes Urias.

I am also grateful to Dr. Thelma Moore-Steward, Dr. Donald Baham, Mr. John Daniels, and Mrs. Glinda Bridgforth-Hodges, who have respectfully given me feedback and encouragement throughout this process.

My eternal gratitude to Walter (Jr.) and Anna Martin, Rev. Robert and Elizabeth Choice, Rev. Wardell and Emogene Johnson, Rev. Dr. Reuben and Dr. Mildred Green, and William and Yvonne Collins for dedicating their lives to educating and teaching Black children. I wish to thank Herman Rankins and Patrice Perkins, who have helped me to develop professionally and personally, and Booker T. McClain, Janine Vaughn, and Richard B. Nash for demonstrating unconditional love and support through the years. I am extremely grateful to my family in Memphis, Detroit, New Orleans, and Akron; and the Bridgeforths, specifically Arilla, Stonewall Sr., Eddie, Ethel, Thomas Sr., Susie, Obie, Stonewall Jr., Lawrence, Sam, Patricia, and Don (D. H.); and my siblings, Joseph A. Hayes, Dr. Patricia L. Clark, and Anita L. Clark. I want to express my gratitude to my in-laws, F. Vincent and Ruby Louque. I am forever thankful to my father, Rev. Jesse Emmanuel Clark, for his protective prayers and spiritual guidance, and my mother, Mrs. Glennie Bridgeforth Clark, who as a single, divorced mother raised four children in the "hood" and gave me great guidance in becoming an educated Black woman.

CONTENTS

TABLES

INTRODUCTION

Honoring Our Need to Speak about Controversial Issues

I N PREDOMINANTLY white colleges and universities (PWIs), an interesting phenomenon often occurs on the first day of class. Unless they have met the professor ahead of time, become familiar with the professor's background via an Internet search or spoken to former students, many students are surprised to learn that they have a Black professor.

This is not only true of some White students but of other groups as well. Black students are no exception. Like their non-Black classmates, few have ever had an opportunity to take a course with a Black professor. The main reason is the small number of Black professors in PWIs nationwide. In *Faculty of Color in Academe: Bittersweet Success*, Turner and Myers (2000) said, "It is widely recognized that minority faculty are severely underrepresented in American higher education. . . . We believe that it is safe to assume that a great many students at predominantly White institutions have had few, if any, classroom experiences with teachers of color" (p. 92).

Another possible reason is that many Americans do not equate intelligence with being Black (Comer, 2002; Drew, 1996; Perry, 2003; Thompson, 2004b; West, 2002; Woods, 2001), a topic that we will return to throughout this book. The media, school curricula, and societal factors have all contributed to a historical and ongoing denigration of "all things black" (Thompson, 2004b), but the Academy has

also played an instrumental role. Therefore, arriving on the first day
of class and realizing that one has a Black professor is at the very least,
a surprise to some students. However, although students in PWIs may
be surprised to learn that they have enrolled in a Black professor's
class, the Black professoriate is not a new phenomenon. The Black
professoriate has had a long history in the Academy and some of the
most influential Blacks in the United States, including W. E. B. Du-
Bois, Carter G. Woodson, Alain Locke, Charles Johnson, James Weldon Johnson, E. Franklin Frazier, and more recently, author bell
hooks and former National Security Advisor and current Secretary of
State Condoleeza Rice, spent some or most of their careers in the
Academy.

In spite of the Black professoriate's long history, especially at Historically Black Colleges and Universities (HBCUs), Black professors,
particularly those who work in PWIs, throughout the nation continue
to struggle for full inclusion in the Academy (Bell, 1994; Childs &
Palmer, 1999; Gregory, 1995; Hale, 2002; Jones, 2001; Mabokela &
Green, 2001; Rankin, 2002; Turner & Myers, 2000; W. Watkins,
2002; White & Siwatu, 2002). As African American women working
at two different PWIs in southern California, this topic is of great concern to us, the authors of the current book. Although we are both
tenured, senior faculty (one at a private PWI, the other at a public
PWI), our quest for full inclusion has been both perplexing and bittersweet. On numerous occasions since we met ten years ago, and eventually developed a friendship, we have discussed our experiences and
most of the topics that are covered in each chapter of this book: respect in the workplace, cultural sensitivity, racism, the hidden "rules,"
the need for a supportive work environment, whether or not we felt
that our contributions were valued, and the ultimate issue of "to leave
or not to leave" an institution.

In the past, both of us have left universities for various reasons.
For example, one of us once worked at a private PWI, where a self-
proclaimed Ku Klux Klan member circulated a note to the other students in the class that said, "Let's get the [N word]!" in reference to

the professor. After notifying her department chair that she was concerned about her safety because the White male student had openly expressed hostility toward her, the chair was unsympathetic. Ultimately, this author ended up having to get a restraining order against the student. From this point on, her relationship with her chair—a White woman who had made culturally insensitive statements to her on several occasions—further deteriorated. This unpleasant relationship affected her interactions with other individuals on campus, including secretaries and program assistants who took the department chair's side.

At the time, this author was the only Black full-time professor in her department and she received little administrative support. Nevertheless, although the campus climate was unwelcoming, she was determined to stay for the sake of the students who needed her support and who valued her as a mentor. These Black students often sought her advice and discussed their problems with her. For example, one day, several of them were distraught when they came to her. They had attended a university event at which the president of the university, a White man who "preached diversity and social justice," and referred to himself as a "recovering racist," had used the "N word" publicly. The author was incredulous. When she checked her voice messages, she had over ten messages from students and other faculty who had also heard the president use the racial slur. She vowed to speak to the president about his culturally insensitive behavior, but her new department chair, a White male, whose philosophy and work centers around cultural proficiency (and who would later become one of her mentors), advised her not to speak with him directly. Instead, she should write a letter and send copies to the chair, dean, and president of the faculty senate.

So, she wrote a letter that expressed her concern about the president of an institution of higher education using the N word in a public forum, and the students' reaction. She also mentioned that White students might feel that it was okay to use the term since the president had used it, and she emphasized how demoralized the Black students had felt.

The president's response turned her incredulity into anger. Not only did he admit that he had used the N word at the event, but he vowed to continue doing so. It finally took the new department chair, and another faculty member, a White female who had been at the institution for over twenty years, to get the president to realize that the use of the N word in public was at the very least, inappropriate. In the end, he wrote a note of apology to the author.

On a subconscious level, this was the beginning of the end for this author, but she decided to bide her time until she went up for tenure. When this happened, she was grateful that the university did the right thing and granted her the tenure that she so deserved. Nevertheless, unlike many professors who would never have dreamed of leaving an institution that had granted them tenure, after the decision was announced, she was even more determined to leave. Several years ago, she left that institution and gave up her tenure to accept a position at a PWI that had more faculty and students of color.

The other author also left an institution because of climate issues. In her case, most of the incidents that culminated in her decision to leave did not pertain to racism or cultural insensitivity; they stemmed from the "hazing" that, in her opinion, is a widely practiced component of "junior faculty boot camp." The junior faculty boot camp that she experienced at a PWI included constant criticism from the department chair. For example, the chair once warned this author that the heels on her shoes were too high to be worn to work. On another occasion, she scolded the author for refusing to permit students (who had not registered even though it was already the first day of class) to enroll in a course that the author was teaching, despite the fact that admitting them would mean that the class size would exceed the university's maximum limit of thirty, and there were not enough chairs in the classroom to accommodate these students. After each tirade, the chair would warn, "Do you want to get tenured? If you do, you'd better listen to me." The more severe aspects of the boot camp entailed the chair's attempts to pit one junior faculty member against the other through innuendoes and often through blatant lies. These experiences were even more painful and perplexing because the chair was an African American woman, who could have served as a mentor and positive role model to women and junior faculty of color.

After consulting several other faculty, the author learned that the chair's tactics were not personal. She had used the same strategies against others, all of whom happened to be women, including several Whites. The difference between the other females who had been subjected to these tactics and the author was that they chose to stay, but after just one year, the author had had enough. When she urged another mistreated woman to leave too, the professor—a Latina, whose hair had started to fall out from stress related to the chair's behavior—said she felt that it was easier to stay than to leave. In other words, the "known workplace," no matter how hostile and unpleasant, was easier for her to deal with than the "unknown." This woman was not alone in deciding to remain in this toxic environment. According to Cloke and Goldsmith (2000), "In most workplaces, people routinely accept humiliation and abuse in order to keep their jobs" (p. 12). However, another woman of color had left the institution shortly before the author was hired, as a result of undermining behavior from this same department chair. Although this professor was happy to have retired from the toxic university environment, she later told the author, "I'm still bleeding from the wounds."

The two aforementioned stories and others like them that we discussed with each other during numerous conversations, led to our decision to write this book. Unlike some of our colleagues who felt that the path of silence and least resistance was the best path to take when problems arose at work, we were unable to do so. According to Bell (1994), "Peace is viewed as a virtue even by those who reject it. Protesters, though, are likely to be denounced as troublemakers by both opponents and friends" (p. xi). Indeed, we have found his words to be true.

During a telephone conversation that we had with each other in

2003, we attempted to brainstorm the reasons why we are driven to speak out even though "Speaking out can result in lost jobs, ruined opportunities, and damaged careers" (Bell, 1994, p. xi). Even worse, according to Lipman-Blumen (2005), "Those who speak out against a leader's decisions during anxiety-ridden times, often bear the wrath of self-appointed watchdogs of conformity" (p. 106). This wrath can include social ostracism in the organization.

Was our need to speak out merely a characteristic of our personalities? After all, both of us are outspoken and opinionated, and some would, undoubtedly, refer to us as "feisty." Was it cultural? As African American women, we were reared to be assertive and to protect ourselves from being victimized. According to Bell (1994), "Protest that can rescue self-esteem is of special value to Black Americans in a society where overt discrimination and unconscious acts of racial domination pose a continual threat to both well-being and mental health" (p. x). Perhaps this was the reason why we felt "compelled" to act and speak out when various aspects of life in the Academy upset us. In *Odd Girl Out: The Hidden Culture of Aggression in Girls*, Simmons (2002) concluded that the Black and Latina girls she studied tended to be more assertive than the White middle-class girls that she studied. In "Shortchanging Girls, Shortchanging America," researchers from the American Association of University Women (AAUW, 1991) concluded that the Black middle school and high school girls in their study had higher self-esteem than the White females. Thompson (2004b) also wrote about the differences between how African American women and White women are socialized.

Obviously, it is unwise to stereotype all Black women as being assertive, having high self-esteem, or as being outspoken, because many do not fit into these categories. In *Rock My Soul: Black People and Self-Esteem*, bell hooks (2003) suggested that like countless non-Blacks, many African Americans, male and female, wrestle with low self-esteem. In *Going Off: A Guide for Black Women Who've Just About Had Enough*, Childs and Palmer (1999) described a study on anger that they conducted. They found that some of the four hundred Black women they surveyed said that in the workplace, they often failed to behave assertively, even when it was in their best interest to do so. "Trying hard not to upset their coworkers or bosses, these women were afraid of the financial consequences of displaying improper anger in the workplace. They avoided confrontations with others even when it was not in their best interest to do so," according to Childs and Palmer (p. 101). However, Childs and Palmer also said that the women in their study who had "advanced degrees had plenty to say about their anger. Sisters have racial as well as gender issues in academia" (p. 107).

As we attempted to understand the forces that compelled us to speak out when others chose to remain silent, we realized that there was no single answer. Culture, how we were reared and socialized, personality, and our history as African American women in a society that historically has denigrated and disparaged Black women were all factors. However, there was another factor. Like Bell (1994) we believed that "Taking a stand . . . can also end harassment and win respect. It can bring about the change you seek for yourself and also for others facing similar hurdles" (p. xi). Furthermore, Lipman-Blumen's (2005) assertion that "Feeling estranged because you differ on the core values that the group embraces can move you to action" (p. 41) resonated with us.

Because of the differences between how we were socialized and how some of our colleagues and "superiors" had been socialized (and undoubtedly for other reasons), we often found that when we voiced our opinions about problems or issues, we were labeled as the "problem child." Similar to what happens in dysfunctional families when one person reveals that "There's an elephant in the living room" or "The emperor has no clothes," instead of addressing the issues that concerned us, sometimes, we found that individuals in positions of leadership used covert strategies to punish or to silence us (Alfred, 2001). Consequently, they missed important opportunities to ameliorate situations that eventually escalated and reached the "dissatisfied enough to leave stage" for us (a topic that we will explore in detail in chapter 1). In *Confronting Authority: Reflections of an Ardent Protester*, Bell (1994) wrote eloquently about the motive to speak out. He stated, "Challenges to those in power are not necessarily motivated by belligerence or hostility, though those emotions may well be present. . . . Rather, those of us who speak out are moved by a deep sense of the fragility of our self-worth. It is the determination to protect our sense of who we are that leads us to risk criticism, alienation, and serious loss while most others . . . remain silent" (pp. ix–x). In "Success in the Ivory Tower: Lessons from Black Tenured Female Faculty at a Major Research University," Alfred (2001) said that although "Getting White academic professionals to listen to the voices of Black women is a particular challenge" (p. 69), among other things, using one's voice can become a means of resisting oppression and becoming successful in the Academy.

Our own experiences and related conversations with each other prompted us to attempt to capture the experiences and "voices" of other Black faculty as well as share our own related stories with a wider audience. Therefore, this book has three targeted audiences: students, faculty, and administrators. First, the book is for any Black faculty members who have ever felt frustrated, dissatisfied, or upset enough to leave a postsecondary institution. However, it is also for Black faculty who are content at their current institutions. We believe that both groups will find quantitative and qualitative data throughout the book that will resonate with their sentiments and their experiences. The book is also for non-Black faculty, and both Black and non-Black department chairs, deans, and others in leadership roles in postsecondary institutions who desire to improve the retention rates of Black faculty. We hope that the book can help them to better understand the experiences and needs of Black faculty. We also hope that this book will help faculty and administrators in higher education become more willing to listen to the voices of Black faculty. As it currently stands, many institutions are not receptive. However, ignoring conflicts and unresolved issues can be extremely costly to organizations (Cloke & Goldsmith, 2000). "Denying the existence of conflicts does not make them disappear," according to Cloke and Goldsmith. "It gives them greater covert power" (p. 11). The high price of unresolved conflicts in the workplace include "litigation, strikes, reduced productivity, poor morale, wasted time and resources, loss of important relationships, divided organizations, and reduced opportunities for learning and change" (p. 2). Finally, we hope that Black graduate students who are considering a career in higher education will find information in this book that will prepare them for the unique experiences, challenges, and rewards that await them.

Because of the strong need for Black faculty, especially in PWIs, this book describes institutional factors that affect Black faculty satisfaction or dissatisfaction at their current institution. Like previous studies and essays (Garcia, 2000; Gregory, 1995; Jones, 2002; Mabokela & Green, 2001; Quezada & Louque, 2004; Turner & Myers, 2000), the book's significance lies in its potential contribution to research seeking to improve the recruitment and retention of Black faculty, particularly at PWIs. Therefore, in this book, we aim to (1) identify the sources of job satisfaction and dissatisfaction among Black faculty; (2) explain which Black faculty are most likely to leave an institution; (3) explain which faculty are most likely to stay, and the related reasons; (4) describe how postsecondary institutions can increase their retention rates of Black faculty; and (5) offer related recommendations to leaders in postsecondary institutions.

Methodology

Participants

This study is based on a self-selected, nonrandom (purposive) sample of 136 Black faculty from various U.S. postsecondary institutions. Females made up 54 percent of the sample. Thirty-six percent of the faculty had been at their current institution for more than six years, and 36 percent had worked at their institution for less than three years. Ninety-one percent of the participants worked at four-year institutions and 59 percent of the participants who worked at four-year institutions worked at public ones. Although the participants represented all of the major regions of the United States, a higher percentage of participants (27 percent) taught in the Midwest, and the two lowest percentages of participants taught in the Southwest (8 percent) and Northwest (5 percent). Fifty-five percent were junior faculty. Although 60 percent were on a tenure track, 54 percent were untenured. All of the major academic departments were represented by the participants, but education faculty represented 56 percent of the sample. Seventy-two percent of the participants had fewer than four Black colleagues in their department and 17 percent were the only Black faculty member in their department.

Data Collection

We collected questionnaires from Black faculty at three professional conferences: the National Association of African American Studies (NAAAS) conference, the American Educational Research Association (AERA) conference, and the National Conference on Race and Ethnicity (NCORE), in 2003. We selected these conferences for two reasons: First, at least one of us planned to attend each conference, which made data collection more convenient. Second, in the past, each conference was heavily attended by Black faculty. This increased the likelihood that we would be able to collect data from a representative sample of Black faculty, so that the results might be more generalizable. At each conference, we, or at least one student assistant, asked Black faculty to complete the questionnaire on the spot. After completing the questionnaire, participants were offered a candle or candy as a token of our appreciation for their time and willingness to participate in the study.

The Questionnaire

We used an original questionnaire that we developed as the primary data source, and interviews as the secondary data source. The questionnaire, which we field-tested, consisted of instructions, a short description of the study, fifty survey items, and a section for additional comments. The first main section consisted of thirty statements that required the use of a four-point Likert scale (4 = strongly agree, 3 = agree, 2 = disagree, and 1 = strongly disagree). The second main section consisted of six questions and statements that required participants to place a check next to items pertaining to their experiences and beliefs about the Academy. The last sections required participants to fill in demographic information and to suggest ways in which the Academy can increase the job satisfaction of Black faculty.

Interviews

We conducted telephone interviews with sixteen survey respondents: seven males and nine females. The average interview lasted twenty minutes. The interviewees lived in California, Florida, Georgia, North Carolina, Maryland, Missouri, Indiana, and Washington, D.C. They worked at community colleges, private postsecondary institutions, public four-year institutions, HBCUs, and PWIs. The interviewees represented tenured and untenured faculty, and positions of lecturer, assistant, associate, and full professor.

Data Analysis

We created and analyzed numerous bivariate correlations and stepwise multiple regression models using SPSS, a standard statistical software program. For each regression equation, we used the questionnaire item that was designed to measure the participants' level of satisfaction or dissatisfaction at their current institution as the criterion variable. The item asked, "What is your current level of satisfaction as an employee at your current institution?" Five options were listed: very satisfied (coded as 5), somewhat satisfied (coded as 4), somewhat dissatisfied (coded as 3), very dissatisfied (coded as 2), and dissatisfied enough to seek employment elsewhere (coded as 1). The predictor variables pertained to whether or not participants had experienced racism and cultural insensitivity, whether or not they felt supported and valued by their faculty colleagues, immediate supervisors (dean and department chair), university-level administrators, and students at their current institution, and other questionnaire items. We used mean substitution for missing data and controlled for collinearity problems by excluding variables that had a tolerance level below .30. To enter an equation, a variable had to be significant at .05 or less. We dropped variables from an equation if their p level was .10 or greater.

Limitations

Although this study has the potential to make a valuable contribution to the existing body of related literature, it has several limitations. The most obvious limitations are the facts that the study is based on a non-random sample, participants from four-year public institutions were overrepresented, education faculty were overrepresented, and some geographical regions were underrepresented. The fact that the participants constituted a purposive sample makes it difficult to ascertain whether or not the results are generalizable. Furthermore, participants were limited to Black faculty who attended three educational conferences, which means that those representing the sciences, mathematics, and other non–social science fields were probably underrepresented in the sample. However, the fact that the participants were diverse in rank, geographical location, number of years as faculty, and the types of institutions where they worked, suggests that it is very likely that the same findings would surface in similar studies. Another limitation is that we did not disaggregate the results to differentiate participants from HBCUs from those at PWIs. However, several questionnaire respondents wrote on the questionnaire that they were employed at an HBCU. Furthermore, the fact that 54 percent of the questionnaire respondents said that the low number of faculty of color at their institution was one of the most difficult aspects of "life" in the Academy for them, and 72 percent said that there were fewer than four other Black faculty in their department, suggests that the majority of the respondents worked at PWIs. More studies that contrast the experiences of Black faculty at HBCUs with their counterparts in PWIs would be insightful, as would studies that contrast the experiences of Black faculty in private PWIs with those of Black faculty in public PWIs. Additional studies that contrast the experiences of Black faculty in PWIs according to the institution's geographical location, and studies that contrast the experiences of senior faculty and junior faculty are also needed. Therefore, there is clearly a need for more work on the topic of "Black faculty retention and satisfaction" to address the ongoing problems of the recruitment and retention of Black faculty, other topics that we explore in this book, and the limitations of our study.

In spite of these limitations, we believe that the results presented in this book can increase Black faculty satisfaction in higher education and thereby improve retention rates, if the "powers that be" in the Academy—policy makers and those in charge of decision making at every level—are willing to listen with open ears. Moreover, we believe that this book can provide Black faculty with a wealth of information to assist them, especially during the times when they are feeling dissatisfied enough to leave their current institution, and Black students with a candid look at the Academy from the perspectives of Black faculty.

TO REMAIN OR TO LEAVE?
THAT IS THE "QUESTION"

Factors Affecting Black Faculty's Satisfaction and Dissatisfaction Levels at Their Current Institution

L IFE IS SHORT. For one of us authors who had three immediate family members (her father, a younger sister, and a younger brother) die before they reached age forty, this statement has become part of the big picture of her life. It's a constant reminder of the importance of enjoying life as much as possible. That includes the part of her life—the countless seconds, minutes, hours, days, weeks, months, and years—that is devoted to her professional career, her job in the Academy. Although life's brevity and the amount of time spent at work are important reasons to have a satisfying job, there are other benefits that can actually affect the quality of one's life. Unhappiness at work can create stress and stress can result in health problems, including cardiovascular disease, musculoskeletal disorders, psychological disorders, workplace injury, suicide, cancer, ulcers, and impaired immune function (National Institute for Occupational Safety and Health, 2005). In addition to medical problems, according to the American Institute of Stress (2005), "Job stress is also very costly with the price tag for U.S. industry estimated at over $300 billion annually" (p. 5). Despite these huge consequences, researchers estimate that 40 to 80 percent of Americans have very stressful jobs (American Institute of Stress, 2005). Undoubtedly, a high percentage of Americans are not as happy or satisfied at work as they could be. In the Academy, job dissatisfaction rates appear to be lower than for the general public but not as good as they could be.

In 2002, the National Education Association (NEA) published "Faculty Satisfaction," a report that summarized the major findings from the National Survey of Postsecondary Faculty (NSOPF). The main conclusion of the report was "The vast majority of faculty members are satisfied with their jobs" (NEA, 2002, p. 1). In fact, "43 percent of part-time faculty members were very satisfied with their jobs [and] 36 percent of full-timers [were]" (pp. 1–2). The main factors that were associated with job satisfaction were faculty's freedom to decide on the content of their courses, opportunities to do outside consulting, and the freedom to decide which courses to teach. Furthermore, "Tenure status did not make much of a difference in terms of overall job satisfaction" (p. 6). The three least satisfying aspects of their jobs were the effectiveness of faculty leadership, not having enough time to keep current in their field, and their salary. In *Faculty of Color in Academe: Bittersweet Success*, Turner and Myers (2000) described the unique experiences of faculty of color. Whereas racism, discrimination, and other manifestations of a nonsupportive work environment led to faculty dissatisfaction, a positive teaching experience, positive interpersonal relationships, being mentored, and strong administrative support increased the likelihood of faculty satisfaction.

Although the NEA report was published in 2002, all was not well in the Academy at that time because during the same year, a controversy erupted that transcended higher education and made national news. Cornel West, one of the nation's most well-known African American scholars, announced that he was leaving Harvard University—the institution whose Afro-American Studies Department West was instrumental in building. The main reasons for West's decision to leave Harvard allegedly stemmed from statements by Harvard's new president, Lawrence Summers, which West perceived as insensitive, and an apparent lack of respect from Summers for West's scholarship and teaching record. Soon, it was feared that other members of Harvard's Afro-American Studies Department would also defect (Roach, 2003). Although most members of the department decided to remain at Harvard, the controversy illustrated the tenuous relationship between Black faculty and the Academy.

More than a decade earlier, another prominent African American scholar was embroiled in a controversy at Harvard that also received a considerable amount of media attention. In that case, Derrick Bell, who, like West, has an impressive publication record that has crossed over to the general public, took a stance at Harvard Law School that caused him to become unpopular with the administration and with some of his colleagues. At the time, Bell, the first Black law professor to be tenured at Harvard, had taught there for twenty years. After realizing that his request that the law school hire a woman of color as a tenure-track faculty member continued to be ignored, Bell took a two-year unpaid leave of absence from the university. When the university refused to grant him a third year-long leave of absence and Bell refused to return, Harvard officials fired him in 1992 (Bell, 1994).

These examples are illustrative of an ongoing problem: for decades, many PWIs have struggled to successfully recruit and retain Black faculty (S. V. Brown, 1988; Hale, 2002). These problems continue to persist. According to Hale, "Attracting faculty of color into the Academy has become an increasingly difficult challenge" (p. 163). For example, during 2001–2002, faculty of color accounted for 15 percent of the faculty in postsecondary institutions, and only 5 percent were Black (National Center for Education Statistics, 2003). There are numerous reasons why many postsecondary institutions continue to have difficulty recruiting and retaining Black faculty. These factors include common hiring practices, the campus climate, and barriers to tenure and promotion.

Mickelson and Oliver (1991) attributed the small number of Black faculty at many institutions to the selection process that is often used for hiring. In addition to the fact that a small percentage of Black PhDs pass through the academic pipeline, the number that will eventually be hired in the Academy is further reduced by the value that is placed on the type of institution from which these individuals graduated. People of color who do not earn their PhDs in elite research-oriented institutions are unlikely to be hired as faculty. The situation is exacerbated by the fact that many Blacks who earn doctorates choose not to pursue careers in higher education, which further reduces the pool of potential faculty (S. V. Brown, 1988).

The overall campus and department climate also affects the recruitment and retention of Black faculty (Hale, 2002; Louque, 1994; Sanford, 2002; White & Siwatu, 2002). According to Carter and O'Brien (1993), a campus climate is "chilly" if one or more of the following factors is present: (1) no formal mentoring system for Blacks, (2) the perception by Black faculty that they are not taken seriously, (3) the belief that the hiring of Blacks meets the affirmative action quota, and (4) the expectation that Black faculty will "fit in" with "White ways." According to Tony Brown (1995), "Often, Blacks in predominantly White settings are rewarded for cultural denial or marginalized further if they associate with other Blacks or express appropriate concern for the Black community" (pp. 219–220). However, Brown also emphasized that when Blacks do this, they do so at a high price: "Acting White is not the same as proving competence. Assimilation is particularly damaging to productivity, because it feeds cultural denial and shifts the focus from meritocracy" (p. 219).

This "chilly environment" has a long history and deep ramifications. Silver, Dennis, and Spikes (1988) found that "There has been a historical opposition to Black scholars in White institutions" (p. 2). D. Olsen, Maple, and Stage (1995) reported that stereotypes about women and people of color in the Academy "are so strong that contrary data about work performance and ability are often ignored in the selection and promotion process" (pp. 269–270). Boice (1993) said that "both women and minorities in professorial roles characterize their experiences in terms like hardship and victimization. These faculty members are often made to feel overworked and inefficient, incompetent, invisible, and unwelcome" (p. 291). Black women faculty seem to experience even more challenges (Gregory, 1995; Louque,

1999; Moses, 1989), for both their gender and their race have historically been viewed as inferior, a topic that we will return to in subsequent chapters.

Mentoring and a perceived lack of support are also important factors that are tied to the campus climate. Boice (1993) found that faculty of color "were almost completely without mentoring, despite
stated desires for someone who could help them find their way
through the labyrinths of campus politics and expectations" (p. 306).
Furthermore, Black professors often have fewer mentoring opportunities than Whites, and many postsecondary institutions do not have
senior Black faculty to serve as mentors and to speak candidly with
Black junior faculty (Association of American Law Schools, 1996).
Unfortunately, in some cases, when institutions do have senior Black
faculty, they are unwilling to serve as mentors, a topic that we mentioned in the introduction and will return to later.

Promotion and tenure practices also affect the recruitment and retention of Black faculty (Gregory, 1995; Silver et al., 1988; Turner &
Myers, 2000), who "are less likely than other groups to be tenured"
(Tack & Patitu, 1992, p. 62). Often, in order to gain tenure, Black
faculty at PWIs have to pay a high emotional price to "play the game"
right and to be perceived as "a good team player" (G. E. Thomas,
1987). However, Boice (1993) found that women and faculty of color
often inadvertently make mistakes during their initial interactions
with their colleagues that seal their doom in a particular institution.

As a result of these problems, Black faculty often find that not
only does the "glass ceiling" still exist, but life in the Academy can be
a lonely, uphill journey (Aguirre, Martinez, & Hernandez, 1993;
Moses, 1989; Tack & Patitu, 1992; C. Thomas & Simpson, 1995;
Watts, 1995). Nevertheless, the presence of Black faculty and other faculty of color is crucial to higher education. The presence of Black faculty sends a message to Black students that they are wanted on campus
and that there are prospective mentors and role models for them there
(Gregory, 1995; Irvine, 1992; Levine, 1993; Louque, 1994). For other

students, this presence is a powerful negator of the stereotype that Blacks are intellectually inferior (Gregory, 1995; Tack & Patitu, 1992).

In order to ascertain whether or not the 136 Black faculty who participated in our study were satisfied at their current institution and planning to remain, we included several related statements and questions on the survey that we created. During follow-up interviews, we asked interviewees to elaborate. In the remainder of this chapter, we present the results describing the percentage of faculty who were satisfied or dissatisfied at their institution, the percentage who planned to remain, and related factors, and we identify the most difficult aspects of life in the Academy for the participants.

Satisfaction and Dissatisfaction Results

The survey results yielded several interesting findings about the participants' level of satisfaction or dissatisfaction at their current institution. At the positive end of the Likert scale, 24 percent of the participants indicated that they were very satisfied at their current institution. At the negative end of the scale, although only 4 percent said that they were very dissatisfied, and 7 percent of the faculty said they were dissatisfied enough to seek employment elsewhere, when the three answers representing levels of dissatisfaction were combined, the results showed that slightly more than one-fifth of the faculty were dissatisfied to some extent (see table 1.1).

Numerous survey items were correlated with the participants' level of satisfaction at their current institution. Several pertained to cultural insensitivity or the institution's racial climate and whether or not faculty felt supported at their institution. When we analyzed several stepwise multiple regression equations, we learned that nine factors (see table 1.2) were actual predictors of the participants' level of satisfaction or dissatisfaction. Senior faculty were more likely than adjuncts, lecturers, and assistant professors to be very satisfied at their current institution. Faculty who had never experienced cultural insensitivity or racism from an immediate supervisor, such as a department chair or

TABLE 1.1
Percentage of Participants Who Were Satisfied or
Dissatisfied at Their Current Institutions

Very satisfied	24
Somewhat satisfied	44
Somewhat dissatisfied	10
Very dissatisfied	4
Dissatisfied enough to seek employment elsewhere	7
No answer	11

$N = 136$

dean, were also more likely to be satisfied than those who had. Moreover, faculty who said that their knowledge about their race and culture were valued by their colleagues, chair, and dean also tended to be satisfied at their current institution. Regarding support, faculty who said that "some non-Black administrators" had been supportive, and those who reported that they had never felt that any administrator was trying to undermine them at their current institution were more likely to be satisfied. Another factor pertaining to feeling supported was that faculty who said that their professional success was important to their colleagues, chair, and dean were likely to be satisfied. Conversely, faculty who said they had frequently felt devalued by students and those who frequently felt devalued by a department chair or dean had a higher rate of dissatisfaction.

Comments from participants whom we interviewed for the study provide more information about factors contributing to their satisfaction or dissatisfaction at their postsecondary institution of employment. An assistant professor who had taught at a university in the Pacific Northwest for nearly seven years explained how a lack of support from her colleagues had contributed to her decision to seek employment at another institution:

> My job is very stressful, and as a result, I feel a lack of motivation and am somewhat disoriented. Recently, a student was very disrespectful to me. When I expressed this fact in a faculty meeting, my

TABLE 1.2
Predictors of Participants' Satisfaction Level at Their Current Institutions

- Senior professors were more likely than adjuncts, lecturers, and assistant professors to be satisfied.
- Faculty who had never experienced cultural insensitivity from a dean or department chair were more likely to be satisfied.
- Faculty who had never experienced racism from a dean or department chair were more likely to be satisfied.
- Faculty who said they frequently felt devalued by students were more likely to be dissatisfied.
- Faculty who said they frequently felt devalued by a dean or department chair were more likely to be dissatisfied.
- Faculty who said their professional success was important to their colleagues, dean, and department chair were more likely to be satisfied.
- Faculty who believed that their knowledge about their race and culture were valued by their colleagues, dean, and department chair were more likely to be satisfied.
- Faculty who had received support from some non-Black administrators were more likely to be satisfied.
- Faculty who had never felt that any administrator was trying to undermine them at their current institution were more likely to be satisfied.

$N = 136$

colleagues felt that it didn't need to be addressed. My colleagues are not supportive and they don't understand the nature of racism or prejudice until it happens to them. One colleague made the comment that "It's just a constant lack of attention or my ability to engage in conversation that may be part of the problem." However, when I called her on it, she thought that I was being rude. Because I'm a part of the Teacher Education Program, I took the conversation from the personal level to a professional level, so she could understand that these issues must be dealt with intellectually and not emotionally.

In addition to complaints about a lack of support from colleagues and administrators, throughout the study, having a low number of faculty of color, especially African American faculty as colleagues, surfaced as an important factor that affected Black faculty satisfaction.

For example, a professor who had taught for several years at a public four-year university in the Southwest said that although she was somewhat satisfied with her institution in general, she was dissatisfied that she was the only African American faculty member in her field. She stated:

> As the only African American faculty member in the College of Education, it is kind of stressful because there is no one else to discuss things with you confidentially, or who shares the level of integrity that I feel I have. Although there are two other African American people who hold staff positions, they are in different departments. I had a hard time finding confidants until they hired more African American faculty. During this past hiring, they hired a Black male. However he is from Africa and that's not the same.

Another interviewee, an associate professor who had taught at a university in the Northwest for more than ten years, said he was dissatisfied enough to leave his current institution. One of the reasons was the low number of African Americans in his department and throughout the university. He explained:

> One of the reasons [for his desire to leave] is a lack of a critical mass. I think that each university I've worked at has a problem with a critical mass of African Americans. I think there is a satisfaction issue to be dealt with. My satisfaction probably would be enhanced if there were more African American faculty, and administrators throughout the university. We need to do a better job at [getting a] critical mass—retaining, and recruiting African American faculty. At this university, I can count the African American faculty on two hands. If you give administration an opportunity to count all the African American faculty, they may take two hands and their feet and your two hands and two feet because they put into that particular count everybody who teaches a class, and that includes [graduate students], which is inappropriate in my opinion. I don't think they do that when they count the White faculty. When they look at the faculty, they look at anybody who teaches. In my mind you should

be [only] taking faculty in that count because those people are in a unique situation. We have an issue with the way we count, but my opinion is if you want to do something about satisfaction, enhance the number of people who are in tenure track and full-time administrative positions who are representing different cultural groups and in my case, African Americans.

Another interviewee said:

Recently my biggest concern has been the hiring policies and practices. I was hired in 1996. At that time, there were no other Black full-time faculty members. The next year, they hired two. Subsequently in 1997, there was no hiring of Black professors in full-time positions. But simultaneously there's been a dramatic increase in the hiring of Asian professors. Vietnamese, Korean, Japanese, Indians, and all kind of Asian backgrounds. Our service area is a community that does have a significant Cambodian population, but other than that, the hiring of the Asian faculty has been extremely disproportional to the community that we serve. Their experience does not include working with urban students, such as the population we have in southern California, which is African American and heavily Latino. So, I'm finding that there is a preference for Asian females. . . . It bothers me. I don't see any active recruitment of African American scholars and in fact, there's not been one African American male full-time on the faculty.

Numerous faculty also spoke about the impact of the racial climate at their current institution on their job satisfaction level (a topic that we will discuss in detail in chapter 6). For example, a professor, who spoke about how students' behavior toward her affected her satisfaction level and who believed that their behavior was indicative of the racial climate at the institution, said:

During my first semester here, I was so stressed that my stomach would be upset on a regular basis. It was one of those things where I was dreading every day because the students were so resistant to me; they were blatantly rude. My first day in class, I had one student question my credentials. First, she asked me how did I become a professor. At first, I thought she was asking how *one* becomes a professor, like she was interested and wanted to know, and so I said, "Oh, are you interested in becoming a professor?" and she said, "No, I just wanted to know how *you* got here." So, this was my welcome on my first day.

Then . . . maybe at the end of that week, I had another student asking if this was an Intro. class that I was teaching, and why I was teaching, and was this the way I was supposed to be teaching, and all this kind of stuff. It was very intimidating. Then, I had another class where the students were again just so rude, walking into the class late, just walking right in front of me and talking to each other while they did it, acting like it wasn't disruptive. They told me to my face that my class wasn't important enough for them and that I shouldn't be giving them so much work because this wasn't an important class for them. You know, just that kind of blatant disrespect, and rudeness. Ironically, the class where I constantly got that was a "Race and Ethnic Relations" class. And the other class where I got the credential question was an "Intro. to Sociology" class, which was ironic because they were trying to tell me about basic social issues. It's like I know this like the back of my hand and you're just getting to college and you're telling me that you know more.

A male interviewee at an institution in Georgia, who spoke about the psychological and physiological effects of his job, remarked:

I can definitely say that it has created stress. In physical and emotional stress, the situation is that basically you're constantly dealing with some type of conflict, or some issue. Whether it be in a personal situation or a professional situation, it's stressful on you mentally. My eating habits are poor; my drinking has increased since I have been working in higher education. You know, I can't get any more specific than "I don't sleep well, I don't eat well, and I know that I am under an undefined amount of stress." I know this. I'm constantly trying to document something, keep up with something. . . . I consider my job to be twice as much paper work as the average person, as a White person, because I'm constantly having to document everything that others do, . . . and constantly having to justify anything that I do that people may question. So, it's constant. It's a lot more damn work. It's too much work. I was going to say something a minute ago and I'm going to add it now: "If this were a marriage—and having been married before and divorced—I would divorce, again. If this were a marriage and not a job—which in many ways is like a marriage—but if this were a legal marriage between a man and a woman, I would file for divorce."

This same professor went on to explain why he actually felt "hopeless" about the racial climate at work:

I hate that you even called me this morning because I've been on the phone all this morning and late last night dealing with some stuff between myself and another faculty member who is a minority faculty who is going through a lot, and I am going through a lot. It seems like everybody in my institution is going through a lot. This is really close to my heart at this particular moment, but my response to that is this: As I sit here now . . . I am thinking about my past two years and my experiences. I can't help but ask myself what I have gotten myself into; why have I put myself in this position and what can I do to get out of this situation? I'm saddened; I'm hurt; I'm disappointed. I feel like I am a better person than this. I feel like I'm a better person than the majority of people that I deal with. I wouldn't treat another human being this way, and I feel hopeless. I feel there is no hope for this situation. I'm beginning to really buy into the idea that this is what it is; it will never be anything different; it will never be any better. There will be nuances of what we as minorities think are improvements or we'll think that something is getting better, but it's really not. I'm beginning to believe that racism is inherent, and that there is nothing that you can do about it. It's like the situation I gave you with the animals sleeping with the enemy type of thing and the most common example that I give is that of animal. I look at Siegfried and Roy, the two circus entertainers rolling around with those damn tigers, and hugging and kissing on those damn tigers, and then they acted so shocked when that tiger almost took that man's head off. My point is this: That is a *tiger*, and that is what *tigers* do. That tiger only did what it was designed to do. Having said that, it just took a bit longer. It didn't just happen instantly. It just took some time, but, you know, that is what tigers do. I think it is almost a genetic, inherent built in factor, that they have to do this to stay in the position that they are in. And that is really scary, because it implies that God designed them that way, and that gets into a whole other issue. I know I've blown your mind with that response, but basically, I just feel like it is a hopeless situation. I'm honestly looking at change, and my change would probably be to a non-White institution; you know, to a minority institution where I know there is a whole other set of issues, but I won't have this one.

Choosing to Remain or to Leave

Although only 7 percent of the participants rated their level of dissatisfaction as "dissatisfied enough to seek employment elsewhere," 38 percent said they did not plan to remain at their current institution indefinitely. Because nearly one-fourth of the participants did not answer this question, the actual percentage who planned to leave may have actually been much higher. It might also mean that these participants were unsure about whether they would leave or remain at their current institution (see table 1.3). Several survey items were correlated

TABLE 1.3
**Percentage of Participants Who Were Planning to Remain
at Their Current Institutions Indefinitely**

Not planning to remain indefinitely	38
Planning to remain indefinitely	38
No answer	24

N = 136

with whether or not faculty planned to remain (see table 1.4). The strongest correlation was related to faculty's level of satisfaction at their current institution. Faculty who were very satisfied were most likely to state that they planned to remain at their current institution.

Several interviewees said they planned to stay at their current institution because they were happy with it in general or happy about some aspect of it. For example, a full professor of education who had taught at a public research university in the Midwest for several years stated, "It is an excellent institution for the kind of work that I do." Another full professor said he planned to remain at the northeastern public university at which he'd taught for less than four years because it offered "good growth opportunities." An associate professor in the Southwest said that he was "very satisfied" and "generally, things are going well." Other participants said they planned to remain at their current institution because they liked the environment, or the work that they were doing, they were having no problems, or they liked the pay.

One of the most frequently cited comments that participants wrote on the questionnaire revealed that their level of satisfaction was related to whether or not they felt their institution was supportive. For example, an assistant professor who worked in the Midwest wrote that he planned to stay because his department was "great and very supportive." A full professor who held an endowed science chair at a private university in the Southeast said she was very satisfied and planned to remain because, "I have found an institution with administrators who understand research." An associate professor who had taught for more than nine years wrote, "I am very lucky to have two diverse and understanding bosses." A woman who had taught for less than four years at a public research university in the West said, "My department is very small and the majority of the faculty of color (Native Americans, Latinos, African Americans) are very supportive." A professor who had taught less than one year at a public comprehensive university stated, "I work with a critical-theory based program where I am protected from a lot of the problems and can effect change." A male

TABLE 1.4
Factors That Were Correlated with Whether or Not Faculty Planned to Remain at Their Current Institutions Indefinitely

Factor	Strength of Correlation		N
Satisfaction level	.54	$p < .001$	$N = 104$
Rank	.36	$p < .001$	$N = 104$
Mentoring students of color was one of the least rewarding aspects of their job.	−.31	$p < .003$	$N = 89$
Tenure track	.25	$p < .012$	$N = 92$
Finding time for research was one of the most difficult aspects of their job.	.25	$p < .02$	$N = 92$
Participants' community service work was one of the least rewarding aspects of their job.	−.25	$p < .02$	$N = 84$
Administrative support was one of the least rewarding aspects of their job.	−.23	$p < .04$	$N = 82$
Participants' research was one of the least rewarding aspects of their job.	−.22	$p < .05$	$N = 88$
Finding time for course prep was one of the most difficult aspects of their job.	−.22	$p < .05$	$N = 84$

who worked in the Northeast at a private four-year comprehensive university said he planned to remain because, "I have relative freedom to do my work."

Conversely, several participants also wrote comments indicating that their plan to leave their current institution resulted from a lack of support. For example, an assistant professor who had taught at a midwestern community college for less than a year said, "It's not where I see myself long-term. The environment is not supportive of my skill set." An adjunct who said he was very dissatisfied at the private four-year university in the West where he taught education courses, said, "There is really no support or understanding for my area of focus and interests."

The second highest correlation revealed that rank was linked to whether or not faculty planned to remain. Senior faculty were more likely than junior faculty to say they planned to stay at their current institution. Numerous participants wrote on the questionnaire that they planned to remain because they were close to retirement. For example, a full professor who taught African American Studies courses at a community college in the West wrote that he was very satisfied and had been at his institution for thirty years. An associate professor of education at a four-year private university said that although she was only somewhat satisfied, she planned to remain at her current institution because "I am five years from retirement." A full professor at a community college in the West expressed similar views. Although she was only somewhat satisfied, she planned to remain because, "I plan to retire in two years," she stated. However, a community college instructor who had taught counseling courses in the Midwest for more than nine years said that she was very satisfied and planned to stay indefinitely because "I think this is where I'm supposed to be until retirement." At least one participant who was close to retirement was considering leaving her current institution. Even though she had tenure at a public four-year university in the South where she taught psychology courses, she rated her level of satisfaction as dissatisfied enough to seek employment elsewhere. She wrote, "I have taught for twenty-five years and I am ready to consider leaving."

Four survey items pertaining to aspects of their work that were the most or least rewarding to the participants were also correlated with whether or not they planned to remain at their current institution. Faculty who said that administrative support was one of the least rewarding aspects of their jobs were more likely than those who found it rewarding to state they were not planning to remain at their current institution. (In chapter 3, we present more details about the importance of a supportive work environment.)

We also learned that faculty who said that their own research and those who said that finding time for research were the least rewarding aspects of their job were more likely to indicate they did not plan to stay. Several participants wrote comments on the questionnaire that provided more information about these findings. For example, an assistant professor who had taught at a northeastern public four-year university for more than six years said he planned to leave because "I am going to a position that will give me more time to do research." An assistant professor who had taught less than one year at a private university in the Northeast said, "Because of a large teaching load, I cannot focus on new research." A lecturer at a southeastern private university said, "I hope to move to a more research-oriented institution within two years." We will return to the topic of time management later in this chapter and in subsequent chapters.

Participants who said their community service work was one of the least rewarding aspects of their job were also more likely to say they planned to leave. Although none of the faculty elaborated on this point on the questionnaire, there are several possible explanations. One possibly is that the participants did not have enough time for community service. Some researchers have found that Black faculty are more likely to invest their time and effort into teaching and providing service to the wider community outside of the Academy. Another possibility is that the participants were dissuaded from doing community service. Although many Black faculty place a high value on service to the "real world," the Academy has a history of disparaging this work. This point is supported by survey data from the current study: sixty-four percent of the participants agreed that community service is less respected than research and publishing. An additional explanation is that the participants equated the community service item on the questionnaire with service to the Academy: attending department meetings, committee involvement, and so forth, and they may have had negative experiences with this type of service that resulted in their ranking community service as one of the least rewarding aspects of their job. We will return to the topic of community service later in this chapter.

One of the most perplexing findings was that participants who ranked mentoring students of color as one of the least rewarding aspects of their job were also more likely to be planning to leave their current institution. The participants' additional comments on the questionnaire provided few definitive explanations. In fact, only one participant wrote additional comments about this topic. This requires us to speculate about the reasons. One of the most obvious is that mentoring may have been too time consuming. After all, Black faculty often "inherit" Black students who never take courses from them but who seek them out for advisement, and moral support, because of their similar cultural backgrounds. Another possibility is the participants may have had negative mentoring experiences that caused this aspect of their job to appear to be unrewarding. Third, the faculty may have worked on campuses at which there were too few students of color to satiate their mentoring goals or desires. For example, an assistant professor who had taught at a midwestern public research university for more than three years said she planned to leave because of the "small number of people of color." After teaching in the Southeast for more than six years, an associate professor of arts and humanities indicated that she planned to leave because, "I think I would like it better elsewhere, where there's more commitment to diversity, a better president and administration, and a more committed institution." (We will present more results about mentoring in chapters 3 and 7.)

A third of the faculty ranked not having adequate time for course preparation as one of the top five most difficult aspects of their job. We learned that these participants were among the faculty who were unlikely to be planning to remain at their current institution. We will say more about this topic later.

Another factor that was correlated with planning to remain or leave was whether or not faculty had tenure-track positions. Participants who did were more likely than those who did not to indicate they planned to stay. For example, an associate professor of arts and humanities at a southeastern public research university wrote, "I am tenured and relatively satisfied at my institution." Another associate professor who had taught education courses for more than six years at a public four-year university said, "I am tenured and trying to make a change for those who will follow me." However, additional comments that were written on the questionnaire indicated that being tenured or being on a tenure track did not guarantee satisfaction or a desire to remain. For example, a previously cited comment indicated that a professor who was close to retirement was dissatisfied enough to seek employment elsewhere. Several other comments revealed that faculty who had taught at institutions for numerous years were planning to leave. In another case, an assistant professor who had taught for less than four years at a public university in the Southwest said, "After I earn tenure, I'm out. [This university] system needs to actively recruit more folks of color, period." An associate professor who had taught at a public university in the Northwest for more than nine years said he was leaving because "It is very stressful and I cannot attain my potential." An untenured assistant professor in the Midwest said she was very dissatisfied and planned to leave because she would not earn tenure: "I will likely not make tenure because I was 'allowed' to teach too many courses to cover for my colleagues." Finally, an untenured, tenure-track assistant professor at a southeastern community college planned to leave because "There are numerous factors that make the fit improper for me."

Additional comments that participants wrote on the questionnaire revealed other factors that affected their decision to leave or remain at their current institution. Some participants were seeking better job opportunities. Others were close to earning a doctorate and wanted a tenure-track position. Several said that even though they were not totally satisfied at their institution, staying there was easier than leaving. For example, an associate professor who had taught at a midwestern public research university for more than nine years said that leaving entailed "too many encumbrances (house, social ties, etc). Also at my age (57), it's too difficult to start over without a comparable salary. I also rely on a saying I heard from my mother: 'Better to deal with the devil you know than the devil you don't know.'" An assistant professor who had taught for less than a year at a public university in the West made a similar statement. Although she was only "somewhat satisfied," she planned to remain at her current institution because, "I've been to other institutions and I have experienced worse treatment." An assistant professor who had taught less than a year at a public research university in the South said she would remain because "I will not let a jealous group of White people run me off."

Another factor that affected decisions to remain or leave pertained to the institution's location such as in the case of an assistant professor at a private research university in the South who rated her level of satisfaction as somewhat dissatisfied. She planned to leave because "I always try to have a plan B (options) and I'm not crazy about the institution or the city in which it is located." Another assistant professor, who had taught in Oklahoma for less than one year, ranked her satisfaction level as very satisfied. However, she planned to leave because she felt "socially and culturally alienated." One of the most succinct but "telling" comments was written by an assistant professor who had taught at a public research university in the Southeast for less than one year. She said she planned to leave because "I am not pleased with academia."

Other Difficult Aspects of "Life" in the Academy

Another questionnaire item asked the faculty who participated in the study to rank the aspects of "life" at their institution that had been most difficult or problematic for them from a list of thirteen options (see table 1.5). Participants also had the option of specifying "other" problems on the questionnaire.

Three of the most difficult aspects of life in the Academy for substantial percentages of the questionnaire respondents pertained to "time." As we stated previously, more than half of the faculty said that finding enough time for research was one of the top five most difficult aspects of life in the Academy for them and two-thirds ranked it as

TABLE 1.5
The Most Difficult Aspects of "Life" in the Academy for the Survey Respondents

Problem	Percent Who Ranked It as One of the Top Five Most Difficult Aspects	Percent Who Ranked It as One of the Top Ten Most Difficult Aspects
Time for research	52	66
Time management	41	57
Low number of faculty of color	36	54
Time for course preparation	33	58
The teaching load	32	55
The racial climate	32	57
Administrative support	25	51
Prejudice against community service	24	44
Mentoring students of color	22	43
Interpersonal relations with colleagues	21	50
Collegial relations with the chair or dean	16	33
A lack of support from other faculty of color	16	37
A lack of support from other African Americans	15	32
Other	5	5

$N = 136$

one of the ten most difficult aspects. Forty-one percent of the respondents said that time management was one of the five most difficult aspects of their work and nearly 60 percent ranked it among the top ten. A third of the faculty ranked finding time for course preparation as one of the top five problems and nearly 60 percent ranked it among the top ten. Another problem that was related to time management was the teaching load of many faculty. Nearly one-third of the faculty said the teaching load was one of the top five most difficult aspects of their job and 55 percent ranked it among the top ten.

Several options on the list of problems that faculty could select on the questionnaire pertained to interpersonal relations and support from administrators and colleagues. One-fourth of the respondents ranked a lack of administrative support as one of the top five problems they faced at their current institution and more than half ranked it among their top ten problems. Sixteen percent said that relations with their department chair or dean was one of the top five most difficult aspects of their job and one-third ranked it among the top ten. Junior faculty were more likely than senior faculty to rank administrative support as one of the most problematic aspects of their job. Faculty who believed their professional success was important to their colleagues, chair, and/or dean were less likely than those who did not to rank administrative support and/or collegial relations with their chair or dean as one of the most problematic aspects of their job. Both problems were linked to the participants' level of satisfaction at their current institution. The faculty who were least likely to say these problems were among the most difficult aspects of their job were more likely to be satisfied at their current institution.

Three problems pertained to the respondents' relations with their colleagues. Although one-fifth of the faculty ranked their interpersonal relations with their colleagues as being one of the top five most difficult aspects of their job, half of the participants ranked it among the top ten. Sixteen percent of the questionnaire respondents ranked a lack of support from other faculty of color as one of the top five most difficult aspects of their job and nearly 40 percent ranked it among the top ten. Fifteen percent said that a lack of support from other African Americans was one of the top five most difficult aspects and nearly one-third ranked it among the top ten. Faculty who had never experienced racism or cultural insensitivity at their current institution were less likely than those who had, to rank any of these three problems as one of the most problematic aspects of their job.

Three other problems also pertained specifically to racial issues. Nearly 40 percent of the faculty ranked the small number of faculty of color as one of the top five most difficult aspects of their job and more than half ranked it among the top ten. Thirty-two percent ranked the racial climate at their institution as one of the top five problems they faced and nearly 60 percent ranked it among the top ten. Twenty-two percent of the faculty said mentoring students of color was one of the top five most difficult aspects of their job and 43 percent ranked it as one of the top ten. Through correlation analysis, we learned that there were three similarities among the faculty who were most likely to rank these three aspects of life in the Academy as being among the most problematic for them. First, these faculty were more likely to say they had experienced racism at their institution. Second, they were more likely to indicate they had experienced cultural insensitivity. Third, they were more likely to say that the racial climate at work had caused stress for them. Faculty who ranked the racial climate as being one of the most difficult aspects of their job were also less likely to be satisfied at their current institution. These faculty and those who ranked the low number of faculty of color at their institution as being among the most problematic aspects tended to work in departments in which they were the only Black faculty member or they had very few Black colleagues in their department.

Finally, nearly one quarter of the faculty said that prejudice against community service was one of the top five problems that they faced and 44 percent ranked it among the top ten. Like many other survey items, racism and cultural insensitivity were correlated with this problem. Faculty who had experienced racism and/or cultural insensitivity at their institution and those who said that the racial climate had caused stress for them were more likely than other faculty to rank prejudice against community service as one of the most problematic aspects of their job. Table 1.5 contains a list of the most difficult aspects of life in the Academy for the questionnaire respondents.

Summary

The results that we presented in this chapter contain some positive and negative news about the Academy from the perspective of the Black faculty who participated in our study. The good news is that nearly one quarter of the participants were very satisfied at their current postsecondary institution and only 7 percent were dissatisfied enough to leave. However, 21 percent of the faculty expressed some level of dissatisfaction and nearly 40 percent did not plan to remain at their current institution indefinitely. As we stated previously, because nearly one-fourth of the questionnaire respondents failed to answer this question, the actual percentage of faculty who planned to leave may have been higher. In the National Survey of Postsecondary Faculty, 43 percent of part-time faculty and 36 percent of full-time faculty were very satisfied with their jobs. Conversely, in our study a much lower percentage of the participants were very satisfied in comparison to the national sample.

We also found that unlike the National Survey of Postsecondary Faculty, for the participants in our study rank mattered (Gregory, 1995; White & Siwatu, 2002). In other words, senior faculty were more likely than junior faculty to be satisfied at their institution. Of course, because senior faculty may feel more secure in their jobs than junior faculty, this finding is understandable. However, in the national study (NEA, 2002), "Tenure status [i.e., being senior faculty] did not make much of a difference in terms of overall job satisfaction" (p. 7).

The fact that time management and time for research surfaced among the most difficult aspects of life in the Academy for some of the participants should not be surprising either. Black faculty often find that more demands are placed on them than their White counterparts (White & Siwatu, 2002). For example, Turner and Myers (2000) found that the faculty of color whom they studied felt they were "expected to work harder than Whites" and felt that "faculty of color must be twice as good to be equal" (p. 90). In addition to mentoring students, teaching classes, course preparation, conducting research, and serving on university committees, they are also expected to be experts on "black issues," and to be involved in the wider community outside of the university (Gregory, 1995; Turner & Myers, 2000; White & Siwatu, 2002). This heavy workload can cause Black faculty to become so overextended that they are unable to devote enough time to their scholarship, which can cause them to be denied tenure and fail to be promoted (White & Siwatu, 2002). According to Turner and Myers (2000), "Faculty of color are involved in a Catch-22; they feel they cannot refuse to serve on committees, but heavy service loads mean less time for the research that is the focus of tenure review" (p. 25).

Like Turner and Myers (2000), we also found that the racial climate and whether or not faculty felt supported were also important factors affecting their job satisfaction and plans to leave. In the two high-profile cases that we cited at the beginning of this chapter, and in the National Survey of Postsecondary Faculty (NEA, 2002), rank did not appear to matter, for although Cornel West and Derrick Bell were both full professors at Harvard, each decided to leave. In the current study, although rank was an important predictor of the participants' satisfaction level, some senior faculty and tenured professors also planned to leave their current institution. What became apparent in the Bell and West cases and in the current study is that the racial climate at work and the extent of institutional support appear to be more important determinants of Black faculty overall satisfaction than rank.

Finally, the results that we presented in this chapter strongly suggest that leaders in higher education—immediate supervisors, such as department chairs, deans, and other administrators—play an important role in whether or not Black faculty are content in the Academy. One quarter of the questionnaire respondents cited administrative support as one of the top five most difficult aspects of their job and more than half said it was one of the top ten. Moreover, most of the nine factors that were predictors of the participants' satisfaction level pertained to their relations with administrators. In the National Survey of Postsecondary Faculty, effective leadership was one of the least satisfying aspects of the workplace for many participants, and Turner and Myers (2000) also identified a link between administrative support and faculty satisfaction. Furthermore, a lack of administrative support was also a key determinant in Derrick Bell's and Cornel West's decisions to leave their institution. These issues, as well as several other factors that are the main sources of dissatisfaction for Black faculty, will surface repeatedly throughout the remaining chapters. In the next chapter, we examine the crucial role that "respect" or lack of respect plays in Black faculty satisfaction or dissatisfaction.

2

ALL I'M ASKING IS FOR A "LITTLE" RESPECT AT WORK

The Importance of Feeling Valued and Respected

DURING THE 1960s, Aretha Franklin's "Respect" became one of the most popular songs of the decade. The song remains popular today and has been sung by many other artists. One of the reasons for its popularity is that it resonates with people. After all, who doesn't want to be respected and to feel valued and appreciated? Although some racial or ethnic groups, particularly White males, may assume that they will automatically be treated respectfully, for African Americans, history has proven that it is naive for us to make the same assumption. The Black professoriate is no exception. In chapter 1, we quoted a professor who spoke extensively about students who questioned her credentials and knowledge, and were openly defiant and disrespectful toward her. Moreover, both of us authors have had similar experiences from some students, colleagues, and administrators. For example, on the first night of class at a PWI, one of us was passing out the course syllabus and other relevant materials, when a group of White students asked, "Aren't you intimidated by us?" When the author replied, "No. Why should I be?" they resumed their conversation with each other and appeared not to think twice about the inappropriateness of their question. At the time, the author wondered if these students would have asked a White professor the same question.

This lack of respect for Black professors appears to be common in

PWIs. Bonner (2004) found that African American faculty often infer that some of their students never really view them as competent. Students routinely question them about their qualifications and many Black faculty believe they must work twice as hard as their White colleagues. Ladson-Billings (1996) described a White professor who noticed the difference between how students viewed him versus how they viewed female faculty of color. According to this professor, students perceived him as being scholarly and objective when discussing class and gender issues, but they viewed women of color as being "self-interested, bitter, and espousing political agendas" (p. 78). Spann (1990) found that women faculty of color were more likely to have their authority challenged than their White male counterparts. Jarmon (2001) said, "As I settled into my teaching role and became comfortable with the organization and content of my course, another issue of concern emerged . . . dealing with students who did not want to be taught by a Black female professor and thus challenged my authority in the classroom" (p. 178). According to Childs and Palmer (1999), "Due to our history in America, Black women have always had to deal with issues of respect. . . . When a Black woman feels disrespected, or dissed, feelings of anger well up inside her" (p. 36). Regarding the Academy specifically, Childs and Palmer stated, "Black women in academia complained about the frustration of not receiving the level of respect that is automatically given to others. Many discussed having to prove themselves as tough or strong women to gain respect inside and outside of the classroom" (p. 107).

However, the problem of disrespect affects Black men as well (Bell, 1994; W. Watkins, 2002; West, 2002). According to West, "To be a Black man in America is to be at risk; to be a Black man in the American Academy is to be subject to unexpected and (usually unwarranted) disrespect" (p. 8). In addition to disrespect, like Black women, Black males in the Academy must contend with behaviors and attitudes that stem from negative stereotypes, but according to West, Black males are also often perceived to be a threat to certain colleagues.

One result of this lack of respect for Black faculty that may directly contribute to job dissatisfaction and the decision to leave an institution is negative teaching evaluations from students, a topic that we will return to in chapter 6. Ostrow (2002) said that "Data indicate that female faculty members face negative bias in the evaluations of students as well as senior colleagues. Many of them will hold you to a higher standard while others—consciously or not—will simply expect you to fail" (p. 1). These words could have also been written specifically about both male and female Black faculty.

Both of us authors have experienced pain and dismay after receiving unfair teaching evaluations. For instance, one of us received evaluations in which students complained about her hairstyle, as well as her style of teaching. One student wrote, "She only talks about Black people and we feel her hairstyle is threatening." At the time, the author was wearing braids. The other author received evaluations from students who complained about the fact that she ate a bag of cheese popcorn in class (the class met from 7 p.m. to 9 p.m. and the popcorn was eaten in lieu of dinner), that she sat down instead of stood when she taught, and that she used the Socratic method of teaching versus lecturing. According to Bell (1994) "Students, though, while not reluctant to complain when a minority teacher departs from the style of White professors—a heresy they see as sufficiently suspect to warrant a trip to the dean's office—remain silent in the face of teaching they consider poor in White teachers' classes" (p. 39). To illustrate this point, Bell described a personal experience. Once while he was substituting for a White colleague, students told Bell that they were disgruntled at the way the course had been going. Bell said, "I was simply a less intimidating figure to whom they felt free to voice their complaints. But when a Black teacher seems less than ideal, students are similarly unintimidated when it comes to end-of-term evaluations" (p. 40).

However, we have also learned that, like White students, Black students and other students of color can treat Black faculty and non-Black faculty disrespectfully. For example, one of us has been criticized and spoken to disrespectfully by some Black students over her expectations and standards. She has also been removed from the dissertation committees of a few Black students and two Latino students, who were more receptive to receiving feedback about their work from non-Black faculty. At a conference that she recently attended, she heard similar stories from several other Black faculty, especially one woman who taught at an HBCU in Texas.

The result, Bell stated, is that unfair or arbitrary teaching evaluations can have a negative effect on tenure decisions, especially when the decisions are being made by White colleagues who are already "suspicious" and skeptical of the qualifications of Black faculty. Hence, the lack of respect that Black faculty may experience in the Academy is not just relegated to students. It can come from colleagues, as Bell noted, who are automatically suspicious of whether or not Black faculty are qualified instructors and, more important, qualified for tenure. As African American professors, we have personally experienced two types of disrespect from some of our non-Black colleagues at various PWIs.

For example, one form of disrespect that one of us has experienced has often stemmed from her dissenting views about standards and expectations for students. She has repeatedly found herself at odds with certain colleagues who believe they are doing graduate students a favor by passing them through the system without holding them to high academic standards. Ellis (2002) said, "Low expectations and racial bias exist on college and university campuses across our nation" (p. 70). One consequence is that students with poor writing and research skills who are admitted into masters, doctoral, and teacher training programs graduate with the same weak academic skills (Thompson, 2004b). According to Toth (2002b), who uses the alias of "Ms. Mentor" in her regular advice column that is published in the *Chronicle of Higher Education*, it is a common practice in higher education for African American students to be held to lower standards. She stated, "Most African-American graduate students, in particular, are not mentored. Too many are passed on, without constructive criticism of their work" (p. 2). Rowley (2000) also observed that this common practice exists in higher education. He called it a negative form of mentoring, which includes the lowering of expectations and advising students to work below their potential. Several Black professors agree that excellence is required for success in the Academy. For instance, Joseph White, an eminent scholar in the field of Black psychology, urged African American males in academia "to be consistent in the pursuit of excellence. If you are going to do something, then be the best you can be. . . . If you are the best that you can be, people will recognize it, and that will protect you from a lot of things" (White & Siwatu, 2002, p. 95).

For acclaimed African American scholar, author, and university president Freeman Hrabowski, the importance of excellence and high expectations for African American students is a recurring message in his work (Hrabowski, 2001, 1999; Hrabowski, Maton, Greene, & Greif, 2002; Hrabowski, Maton, & Greif, 1998). In the article "Embracing Excellence and Diversity," he said, "we need to set high expectations for our students and ourselves as we strive to ensure the success of all students in the future" (Hrabowski, 1999, p. 5). Hrabowski not only pays lip service to this message about the importance of excellence and high expectations for students of color, but through his Meyerhoff Scholars Program, he has demonstrated what can happen when the message is operationalized. The Meyerhoff Scholars Program has "become one of the nation's leading producers of high-achieving African American students going on to graduate and professional study and careers in mathematics, science, and engineering" (Hrabowski, 2001, p. 26).

In our opinion, as authors, researchers, and African American faculty, the underlying assumption that drives this practice of low standards and low expectations for African Americans is the widespread belief that certain students, especially African Americans (Thompson, 2004b) and Latinos, are incapable of doing quality work. In other words, we believe that K-12 teachers and professors in the Academy who merely "pass them through" the system really harbor racist and deficit beliefs about the students' aptitude. This practice of lowering standards is harmful to students because it gives them a faulty assumption about their abilities, the value of the degrees and credentials they have "earned," and it sets them up for failure in the workforce (Thompson, 2004b). Graduate students who are subjected to inequality of educational opportunity through low teaching standards and expectations can become junior faculty who are unable to gain tenure as a result of poor research skills and low writing productivity. Moreover, this common practice also hurts higher education. Recently, the Academy has come under public scrutiny and criticism for indulging in grade inflation and the prevalence of "diploma mills." When students are permitted to "buy" grades and degrees, it harms the reputation of all members of the academic community. Nevertheless, the author in question has learned that it is a waste of time to discuss the practice of holding students to low standards with some colleagues. The end result has always been that her words have fallen on deaf ears and the status quo has been maintained to the detriment of students of color and the Academy's reputation. It has also resulted in some of her colleagues dissuading students from taking her classes and discouraging them from asking her to serve on their dissertation committees.

A second form of disrespect that the aforementioned author has experienced from some colleagues has repeatedly manifested itself at PWIs during department meetings and when important decisions were being made. At the time, she was usually the only African American professor in the department or one of only two or three Black professors. The usual scenario was that, like her colleagues, the author would share her views and opinions about topics that were being discussed and policies that were being considered. With the exception of one or two colleagues who made no attempt at politeness or patience, most would listen politely to her opinions. Then, business would resume as if she had never uttered a word. It appeared that what she said "went in one ear and out of the other." When, and if, a vote was taken, she usually found herself as the lone dissenter. If she had expressed her views with passion and emotion, some colleagues would later justify their discounting and disparagement of her opinions by saying "She's problematic." However, her mentor recently reminded her that "there have been times when [her] viewpoint not only was heard and respected but carried the day."

Nevertheless, over time, this author eventually realized two important points: (1) her opinions were really unimportant to most of her colleagues—even those who appeared to listen attentively to what she had to say—and (2) although she was a tenured professor, when it came to decision making, she was not a "key player" and perhaps—despite her status as a tenured senior professor—not a "player" at all in such departments. These experiences also caused the author to feel "congenially disrespected" by some of her colleagues. They were polite. They listened to her. However, their actions shouted: "Our knowledge base, views, and opinions are superior to yours and we will make decisions—even those that affect you and your students—accordingly." William Watkins (2002) described similar experiences that he had with colleagues. When this type of paternalistic, condescending behavior that is based on the supercilious belief that "We know what's best" and "You know little that we should take seriously" becomes the norm in a department where there is only one African American professor or a number too small to constitute a critical mass, the professor can choose among several options. She can keep fighting a losing battle, choose to stop attending department meetings, or she can become dissatisfied enough to leave that particular institution. We will say more about this "culture of arrogance" that permeates the Academy in chapter 7 and in the conclusion.

In addition to faculty and students, disrespect toward Black faculty can also come from staff and administrators as well. In fact, disrespect and the "chilly climate" that permeates many PWIs from the vantage point of Black faculty are related. Phillip (1995) provided a pertinent example in which "a nationally recognized African American female professor of English was publicly affronted by an older, white administrative aide to the Department Chair" (p. 18). After the professor asked why her office was being used by someone else without her permission, "The aide raised her voice, pointed her finger, and slammed the door in the face of the professor" (p. 18). In addition to other staff members, students witnessed this incident. When the professor asked the department chair to "support her efforts to obtain a formal apology from, and a reprimand of record for the aide" (p. 18), she was disappointed. This disappointment triggered her decision to leave the institution. Phillip (1995) wrote, "In her letter of resignation from the department, the professor, who is tenured" (p. 18) said, "My emotional and psychological health is suffering, and the attention that I normally devote to my work and my students has lagged. . . . I feel that I am not welcomed in my [departmental] 'home.' I can no longer retain respect and dignity as an African-American woman professor in a department where I can, with impunity, be subjected to such treatment" (p. 18).

This story illustrates two important points: First, disrespect and respect appear to be important factors that affect Black faculty satisfaction or dissatisfaction at their institution of employment. Second, administrators' responses to complaints from Black faculty can exacerbate or ameliorate situations. An incident that one of the authors of this book experienced is a good example.

In September 2003, the author was teaching a Saturday class for doctoral students, when a staff member, a young White student who worked at the university part-time, appeared at her door and asked to speak with her outside. The student worker proceeded to tell the author that she was in the wrong classroom and needed to move immediately. According to the student worker, another individual was scheduled to teach in the classroom at 9 a.m. Because the class had been in session for thirty minutes, and students had already set up their computers, the author suggested that the student worker simply arrange to have the other individual teach in the other classroom, especially since he had not even arrived on campus yet. But the student worker was adamant, and insisted that the author move her class immediately. When the author said that she would not uproot her students and move just because of someone else's scheduling error, the student worker became incensed. Then, in one of the most blatant displays of "white privilege" the author had ever seen, the student worker said, "I'm going to call security!" She turned on her heel and hurried in the opposite direction. At that point, the author was stunned. Momentarily, her future flashed before her eyes. She visualized the evening news broadcasting a headline story: "Black professor arrested for intimidating young White student," and she envisioned herself in handcuffs, sitting in jail in her brand-new cranberry-colored suit. At that point, she called out to the student worker, "Okay, I'll move my students" (Thompson, 2004b).

When her students learned they would be uprooted and the reason why—security would be called on their professor—they were incredulous. Once they moved to another classroom, the author had difficulty regaining her composure. At one point, she exclaimed to her students, "Only in America!" Eventually the class discussion resumed, but the morning dragged on at a snail's pace. When the moment she had been waiting for—lunchtime—arrived, the author hurried to her office and sent a strongly worded, detailed e-mail to the university's president and to the provost. In addition to recounting what had happened, she wrote that she felt disrespected and felt that the incident was racially motivated. In her opinion, no one at that university, especially a young student worker, would ever dream of threatening to call security on a tenured White male professor. In fact, a Latina graduate student later told the author that in the past, two of her other professors—a White male and an Asian male—had also refused to move when asked to in the very same building where the aforementioned incident had occurred, yet no one had threatened to call security on them.

After this, the incident could have been handled in various ways. The administrators who received the author's strongly worded e-mail could have told her that she was overreacting. They could have accused her of "playing the race card," a phrase that she detests. In other words, they could have demonstrated insensitivity and a lack of support in numerous ways. However, they chose to take the matter seriously. By validating her experiences, apologizing for the student worker's inappropriate behavior, asking the author for suggestions as to how the situation could be resolved, and getting key personnel involved, they ameliorated a situation that could have been blown out of proportion, given that a classroom full of students—including several students of color—were aware that a Black professor had been treated as if she were a criminal. Consequently because of the strong support from the president and provost, the author went from being upset enough to actually plan to leave the institution, to deciding to give the university another chance to prove that it was serious about improving the campus climate for women, faculty of color, and students of color.

Because the issue of respect is so important to Black people at every level of American society, we wanted to learn more about Black faculty's related experiences in the Academy. Via the questionnaire for the current study, we gave participants opportunities to share feedback about whether or not they felt respected and valued at their current institution. The survey items pertaining to respect and feeling valued can be grouped into four main categories: (1) respect from people, (2) respect for participants' scholarship, (3) respect for participants' other contributions, and (4) respect for their race and cultural background. Faculty who participated in the interview phase of the study elaborated on these topics. We present the results in the following section.

Respect for African American Faculty

The majority of faculty who completed the questionnaire disagreed that at their current institution it is common for African American faculty to be treated less respectfully than other faculty, but 45 percent agreed. Nearly 40 percent of the faculty who indicated that this was a widespread practice had worked at their institution for ten or more years and 53 percent were tenured. Through data analysis we learned that the overwhelming majority of these individuals had experienced cultural insensitivity and racism from other faculty, administrators, and students. Most said that racism was common at their institution and that the racial climate at their institution had been stressful for them. Moreover, 87 percent said that there were fewer than four other African Americans in their departments. Although the majority said they were somewhat satisfied, 52 percent indicated that they did not plan to remain at their current institution. One professor, who had seriously considered leaving, said that problems with some of her White colleagues and the way in which her immediate supervisor responded had caused her to become dissatisfied. However, in the end, she was glad that she chose to remain. She explained:

When I brought in several Black faculty from the Black Studies Program last spring, for a presentation, that was the first time, probably more than five Black professors were in that college at one time, at least in my eight years being there and others have told me they haven't seen it in over a decade. So it does affect my job satisfaction. I'm finding that I need to reach outside the college more, much more than I had expected, to find compatibility sometimes in people who share the concerns and issues I do.

It has caused stress for me, not such that it would cause me to leave. At one point I was inquiring to leave because of the relationship and problems with the White female professors. I decided that I needed to work through it. . . . I am satisfied. I'm happy that I decided to stay and not leave the institution. I did begin to look for jobs outside of the university but I'm glad I decided to stay and work through it because I think it's important that African Americans have a presence. Now, I've earned enough seniority to have opportunities to serve on major committees, committees of influence, to have impact and to increase my visibility—I hope making it easier for the next African American person and subsequently I've obtained tenure.

I am not satisfied with the way my supervisor handled that situation that extended over a period of about a year. I'm very dissatisfied. I think it's important that we take a stand against their insensitivity and their preferential treatment of some colleagues over others.

Respect for Their Cultural Background and Race

Sixty percent of the participants said that their cultural background and race were respected by their colleagues, chair, and dean, but 40 percent disagreed. Through regression analysis, we identified three actual predictors of how participants responded to the statement about respect for their cultural background and race. Professors who had never experienced any cultural insensitivity from their colleagues, professors who said they had never experienced any racism from their chair or dean, and professors who said they were very satisfied at their current institution were more likely to believe that their cultural background and race were respected.

Feedback from faculty who participated in the interview phase of the study suggested that some colleagues and administrators were more respectful of Black culture than others. For example, one interviewee said that the president of his university "is not there yet and I am. I'm more new school; he's old school. I have a new perspective. He's stuck in the past from freedom fights and doesn't respect the culture of African Americans. He has a way different approach." Another interviewee complained about his department chair: "He doesn't recognize anything," he stated. "He does not show respect. However the division chairperson gives more respect." A third professor said, "My cultural background and race are respected by my colleagues. As far as the chair, I don't think she is aware enough to even understand who I am or what I'm doing yet."

A related survey item stated, "At my institution, my experiences are valued and respected by my colleagues, chair, and dean." Sixty-two percent of the faculty agreed with this statement and 38 percent disagreed. A regression equation produced two predictors of how participants responded to this statement: satisfaction level and the specific culprit of cultural insensitivity. Faculty who had never experienced cultural insensitivity from their faculty colleagues, and faculty who were very satisfied at their institution were more likely than others to say their experiences were valued and respected.

One interviewee said, "Yes, I think very, very strongly that my cultural background is valued. I think again it has probably to do with the background or expertise that I bring to the table . . . as opposed to my race. I'm in a leading administrative position here, one of very few administrators in this unit or college, so I can't think of any time where I've had any reason to think it was because of my race. If my decisions and thoughts were not accepted, it was because of something related to the content of it, as opposed to my racial background." Another professor said that his experiences are respected to the point that it is "sometimes, too much." He explained:

> We have had an incident on campus where someone came from another campus and started an altercation on our campus. In an effort to be proactive and to not have anything like that happen again, they formed a task force against college violence, and because of my expertise, I was named to be one out of six. Anytime it's something significant or something that they believe that I have experience in, whether it be university wide . . . or departmental, when there are sometimes questions of legality or something that they will touch bases on, they have no problem coming to me with a question, or at least asking my opinion on it.

Knowledge about Their Race and Culture

A third questionnaire item stated, "At my institution, my knowledge about my race and culture are valued by my colleagues, chair, and dean." Sixty-six percent of the respondents agreed with this statement, but one-third disagreed. Again, regression analysis revealed that the predictors of how faculty responded pertained to cultural insensitivity and their satisfaction level. Faculty who were very satisfied at their current institution were more likely to state that their knowledge about their race and culture were valued by their colleagues, chair, and dean. Moreover, professors who said they had never experienced cultural insensitivity from their colleagues, and faculty who said they had never experienced cultural insensitivity from their chair or dean also tended to believe that their knowledge about their race and culture was re-spected and valued. Numerous interviewees provided more details about questionnaire responses to this statement. A professor in the South who said that several incidents led her to conclude that her knowledge about her race and culture was valued stated:

> Just yesterday, I delivered my completed diversity booklet and my colleagues and administrators were commenting that "I don't know how you were able to pull together this diversity booklet." I can see where they are trying to pull people in. They showed me that they respect what I do. Later, I gave a presentation on the chapter for accreditation. It was organized and I had stage presence. Last month, I received fairly positive stroking from the new President of the Association of Teacher Educators [in her state].

A professor who said that she was consulted about issues pertaining to Blacks during Black History Month said:

> During Black History Month, there are a lot of activities going on, or sometimes when there is limited access to Black faculty, I am called upon as an expert almost. I don't know if just having pigmentation can make you some "expert." I may not have studied some of it, but I think that the association or the assumption that I know everything there is to know about Black people is sometimes laughable, and I would not want to ever be recognized as the spokesperson for any Black group, organization and/or persons, but sometimes, we find ourselves in those positions.

Another interviewee described similar experiences. His advice was sought, he said.

> Absolutely, in most situations when it's dealing with any issue of diversity regardless of the conflict. I've been called to be an expert . . . in terms as to how to assess different issues and one thing about my university is that things that deal with African Americans specifically such as Black History Month, and Martin Luther King, are

such valued events on campus, from our chancellor down to many of the top administrators to the point that I need to tell them that we need to celebrate some of the other cultures too. So, we're actively celebrating the cultural appreciation of the Latinos and Native Americans; we're doing a lot of those things.

A professor who described herself as "the local authority" on diversity remarked:

Our campus is heavily populated with immigrants, Blacks from the Caribbean, from West Africa, and Afro Latinos. As a Black immigrant myself, I'm almost the local authority. In instances of student aid and our secretarial staff not working together, the dean, actually in one of our meetings, asked me if I could give my input on what I thought might be going on. So, while they respect my insight, I have to remind them that, "That's what I think, but I am not the authority." It goes back to what I said earlier: "Just because I'm Black doesn't mean I can go and do research on Black people and they'll be happy." It's a double edged sword.

This same professor also added:

There's instruction on campus that is [resulting in] a series of placement tests for our ESL students. The faculty have not been involved in the selection of these assessment tools, so in a couple of meetings we were discussing . . . our plan to counter this decision. I brought up a couple of issues about culture, and it was not the usual discussion on cultural bias, but that since we were going to a computerized testing method that we may inadvertently be working against African males, because back home, it's girls who take typing, not males, and when we put them on a computerized test, they're going to sit there and hunt and peck and not finish the test quickly. So this is a time where the technology may actually work against a group simply because of their own cultural traditions. There was a moment of silence, you know, because this didn't occur to any of them.

Respect for Their Contributions

Two questionnaire items gave Black faculty an opportunity to explain whether or not their professional opinions and contributions were valued and respected. Two-thirds of the respondents agreed that their contributions were valued by their colleagues, chair, and dean, but 30 percent disagreed. Regression analysis identified two predictors of the professors who were more likely to agree that their contributions were valued. Faculty who were satisfied and faculty who had never experienced racism from their chair or dean were most likely to state that their contributions were valued at their current institution.

A number of the interviewees described their experiences and views related to why they felt that their contributions were or were not valued at their institution. One professor said:

> Yes, I do strongly agree that they do value my professional contributions and service contributions. I don't know about any one particular incident, but I'm constantly getting "thank you for coming to do that. We really appreciate you for supporting us in this way, and coming to do this event, and doing a guest talk at this event." So, I'm constantly getting thank yous for my contributions. Then, they have these little appreciation award things at the end of the year, that I'll get from student organizations or the Multicultural Office and the Student Affairs Office, and that sort of thing. "Thank you for your contribution this year to furthering our office's issues and the things we are trying to do in our courses," and that sort of thing.

Another interviewee explained how the value placed on his professional contributions created other opportunities for him. He said:

> You are probably familiar with the McNair Scholarships. I was asked to do a presentation, or be part of a panel on one occasion and was sharing the microphone with five other people, which meant not having much time to talk, but I was one of [the two] African Americans there. But my comments, I suppose, were very well received. I received numerous e-mails the next day about my comments and

interestingly enough, the day after that discussion, I was called and invited to do the keynote presentation for a banquet during the summer, and I have been asked to do several other things relevant to that type of audience. Speaking to African Americans, speaking about cultural issues comes out of comments of others who heard me speak at that panel and that type of thing. I think it is an acknowledgement of at least some type of respect for my ability to speak about cultural issues as they relate to poverty, African Americans, and that type of thing.

Conversely, an interviewee who believed that his contributions were not valued, remarked:

I think for the most part, my contributions are marginalized, like I am marginalized. I think that I'm very, very active on my campus, so it is kind of hard to ignore what I am doing, but within my exact department, it is seen as something that is busy work. It is seen as not really of importance and then what I see in opposition to that is my colleagues really, really, putting a lot of emphasis on what they are doing—in other words, what they view and value. I think we are talking about values here, and that there is less value for my contributions as opposed to [those of] my White colleagues. There seems to be a greater value for what they do and their efforts and their contributions, than for mine. Mine is okay; it's all right, but what's really important is what so-and-so did.

A professor who said that her contributions were valued by some of her colleagues but not the dean and her department chair, explained:

My contributions are valued by some of my colleagues, but my chair and dean, I think, value me only in that they know that I can be counted on to do what I'm supposed to do. I don't think they value my contributions in such ways that I would be selected when the discretionary appointments to do things, like appointments and assignments are made, for instance, when a major grant is awarded to the college. I have not been selected to work on some of those grants, where professors of lesser experience have been. I think my dean is uncomfortable with outspoken people, not meaning that I'm out speaking to people all the time, but because I am willing to speak up. I think she's uncomfortable with people with big voices. I think she likes elementary [school], softer personality types, which I find very interesting. My experiences are valued and respected by my colleagues.

Respect for Their Professional Opinions

In addition to speaking about their contributions, participants also discussed whether or not their professional opinions were valued and respected. Seventy-four percent of the questionnaire respondents said their professional opinions were valued and respected at their institution. Twenty-three percent disagreed. Through regression analysis, we identified two predictors of faculty who were most likely to say their professional opinions were valued and respected. Faculty who were very satisfied and faculty who had never experienced cultural insensitivity from their department chair or dean were more likely than others to state that their professional opinions were valued.

Several interviewees explained why they believed or did not believe that their professional opinions were valued and respected at their institution. A professor at an HBCU said she believed that her opinions were respected at both PWIs and HBCUs. She stated, "Yes, they respect it, and often ask me for articles that I have written on specific topics. At both Black and White institutions, my contributions are valued. On issues of equity I am often asked my opinion."

Another interviewee said her opinions were valued and respected by some individuals but not by all. She said:

I don't know that my professional opinion is valued or respected by the administrators. I think my colleagues do respect what I have to say and what I do. I have not been mentored while I was there. I think that contributed to my slow exit out of the gates to the scholarly writings and publishing I need. I noticed that each of the other two women hired with me had inside connections prior to their appointment. I didn't know anyone, and I wasn't mentored voluntarily by anyone. I tried seeking outside mentoring with a woman at a university in another city, which did help to have someone there to serve as a mentor to attach me to some grants and to work with me on writing. So I didn't have that kind of support and I think it is really important.

One interviewee provided several examples of why his professional opinions were valued and respected by stating:

> I think that they are valued because I brought something so new, some new experiences whereas I've been able to create different programs on the campus where I could more or less open up a cultural center. I think my expertise in terms of how I've helped to embrace differences and educate the campus in terms of the understanding of diversity across the board has been valued. . . . Last semester, I received an award . . . because of my ability to promote cultural understanding and an appreciation of diversity, from the faculty organization, which was recommended by my boss, and my direct supervisor, and our vice chancellor.

A professor who believed two administrators valued his opinions said, "That's the icing on the cake. Yes, in my opinion [the dean] does respect me. The associate dean is sincere. She provided me with a letter of recommendation, and stated that I'd made valuable contributions to our department. She's articulated and indicated by her actions that I am valued." Similar remarks were made by an interviewee who said, "Absolutely. They seek me out and tell me, 'I have such and such a situation,' and they'll ask for my opinion, what I think about a planned course of action. This will actually be due to leadership. The president is a visionary and very proactive, not reactive." Similarly, another professor said, "They ask my advice about everything. I'm the chair for the Governance Committee, and last year I was the co-chair. Further, I'm a member of the Curriculum Committee and I strive to be superior in all areas. When I write something, they all want to read it, and I am valued as a colleague."

An interviewee who realized the uniqueness of her experiences said, "Yes, my situation is strange because half of the staff as well as the administration have all talked to me. They'd like me to co-author a chapter of one of the school's accreditations, and I'm beginning to do more now than I did before." However, a professor who received support from some members of the campus community but not administrators remarked, "Yes, I am valued more so by students and peers, as opposed to administration, which may be the reason I'm leaving." Table 2.1 presents the quantitative results regarding the percentage of faculty who felt respected and supported.

Summary

Webster's Universal English Dictionary (2004) defines "respect" as "to feel or show esteem or regard to" and to "treat considerately" (p. 242). It defines "disrespect" as "rudeness" and a "lack of respect" (p. 90). The results that we presented in this chapter underscore several important points about the participants' experiences related to respect and disrespect. As we illustrated via the questionnaire and interview data, disrespect can be subtle or overt. It can come from staff members, students, colleagues, or administrators. It can surface as a disregard or a lack of value placed on one's knowledge, ideas, or contributions (Turner & Myers, 2000; W. Watkins, 2002), or as an ethnocentric superiority complex (Akbar, 2002; Hilliard, 2002; W. Watkins, 2002) that implies that non-Blacks, especially Whites, are superior to Blacks in every way—the "culture of arrogance" (Thompson, 2004a) that we describe in chapter 7 and in the conclusion. Regardless of the many guises in which disrespect can come, the clearest message emanating from the data is that in order to be content at their postsecondary institution, Black faculty must be treated respectfully by all members of the academic community.

As we stated previously, both of us, the authors of this book, have

TABLE 2.1
Questionnaire Results about Feeling Respected and Valued

Questionnaire Item	% Who Agreed	% Who Disagreed
African American faculty are less respected than other faculty.	45	55
The research of African Americans who specialize in African American issues is less respected than other research.	49	51
At my institution, my contributions are valued by my colleagues, chair, and dean.	66	30
At my institution, my experiences are valued and respected by my colleagues, chair, and dean.	62	38
At my institution, my cultural background and race are respected by my colleagues, chair, and dean.	60	40
At my institution, my knowledge about my race and culture are valued by my colleagues, chair, and dean.	66	33
At my institution, my professional opinions are valued and respected.	74	23

$N = 136$
Note: The difference in percentage totals that are less than 100 can be explained by the number of respondents who failed to respond to certain statements.

experienced various forms of disrespect from some students, colleagues, staff members, and even from a few administrators. At times, depending on the culprit, the context, and outcome, the disrespect had a short-term effect on our morale. At other times, the effect was long term. In a few extreme cases, the disrespect and how it was handled upset us enough to make us seriously consider actually leaving the institution where it occurred. After working hard to earn our doctorates and jumping through all of the hurdles that were required for us to gain tenure, as African American women, we have decided that at the very least, we must be treated respectfully at work. We treat others respectfully, so why should we settle for less? Therefore, like many of the participants in our study, for us, respect is not an option; it is a must.

The results that we presented in this chapter indicate that although most of the participants felt that their contributions were valued, and their race, culture, professional opinions, knowledge about their race and culture, and their background experiences were respected, at some institutions the respect that Black faculty deserve is lacking (Turner & Myers, 2000; W. Watkins, 2002; West, 2002). Nearly half of the questionnaire respondents said that at their institution, African American faculty are less respected than other faculty, and the research of African American faculty who specialize in African American issues is less respected than other research (Smith, 1995; Turner & Myers, 2000; W. Watkins, 2002; White & Siwatu, 2002). These results suggest that many institutions are doing a good job of increasing the likelihood that Black faculty will feel that they are fully accepted in the Academy, but other institutions need to continue to work on the areas that surfaced as problems.

In "Is Congeniality Overrated?" Bugeja (2002) made several interesting observations about the ways in which disrespect can surface in academic departments and schools and differentiated between "congeniality" and "collegiality." In congenial academic departments, Bugeja said, "Faculty members are friendly and agreeable, acknowledging the contributions of their peers across academic ranks" (p. 2). In collegial departments, "shared governance is mindful and inclusive" (p. 2). After studying four types of academic climates (collegial and congenial, collegial but uncongenial, congenial but uncollegial, and uncollegial and uncongenial), Bugeja concluded that the collegial, uncongenial model is best. He explained:

> the working environment might be unpleasant at times and challenging, but the culture of steadfast shared governance—mindful of contrary viewpoints—sharpens both teaching and research, because

professors have something to prove. . . . Moreover, such units usually are as multicultural, interdisciplinary, and politically diverse as the viewpoints of faculty from dissimilar demographics, psychographics, and lifestyles. . . . In sum, the focus is on professional respect (p.3).

When this professional respect is present, students, faculty, and the entire institution benefit. In too many institutions, the reality, however, as Bugeja wrote, is that "Professors of diverse backgrounds or heritages typically feel like token representatives, not because they or their accomplishments go unacknowledged, but because their ideas seldom influence key decisions"(p. 3).

In this chapter, we have presented evidence suggesting that respect and disrespect are factors that are tied to whether Black faculty are satisfied or dissatisfied at their institution and whether they plan to leave or remain. Respect or the lack of respect for Black faculty can come in different forms and from different constituents of the Academy. From students, disrespect can come in the form of negative teaching evaluations and disrespectful behavior. From colleagues, disrespect can come from lower standards for Black students (Jones, 2002; Toth, 2002b) and displaying a pattern of condescending comments and other offensive behaviors that contribute to a lack of full inclusion. Disrespect can also come from staff and administrators who fail to respond to complaints from Black faculty. In summary, we have learned from our own experiences, from the survey data, and from the interview participants that being disrespected in the Academy can result in a Black faculty member becoming dissatisfied enough to leave. In the next chapter, we discuss the importance of a supportive work environment, a topic that is both directly and indirectly related to the need to feel respected in the workplace.

3

WANTED: A SUPPORTIVE
WORK ENVIRONMENT

I N September 2004, one of us authors ran into one of her graduate students, a young White woman, who had come to the university to deliver papers that were related to her dissertation. At the time,
the graduate student was employed full-time as an untenured assistant
professor at another private PWI nearby. When the author asked how
things were going, the student replied enthusiastically, "Great! I love
my job." In previous conversations, the graduate student had shared
specific details with the author about various aspects of her work environment. When combined, the reasons why she loved her job could
be summarized in one sentence: "She worked in a supportive environment and believed that her colleagues and immediate supervisor were
committed to her professional success." In other words, she had
learned one of the main ways that the Academy can increase faculty
satisfaction.

Throughout our years as professors, we have learned some important lessons about support or the lack of it at each of the PWIs where
we have worked. Like respect and disrespect, support can come from
any segment of the university community: staff, students, colleagues,
or administrators. It can be weak or it can be strong. It can occur
periodically, or it can be consistent. The main lesson that we have
learned, however, is that in order to succeed in the Academy and to
feel at least somewhat satisfied, we need consistent and strong support,
ideally from our colleagues and administrators, but at the very least,

from our immediate supervisor. In the past, when this support was lacking, both of us became dissatisfied enough to leave various institutions. In the cases where we had strong and consistent support from our department chair or dean, it was easier for us to deal with other institutional factors that made our jobs unpleasant to some extent.

For example, while working at two different PWIs that had very few faculty of color, each of us had immediate supervisors who were supportive and served as mentors. These supervisors, Dr. David E. Drew and Dr. Randall Lindsey, are White men who have devoted their academic careers to conducting research about social justice and diversity issues. Unlike many liberal Whites in higher education who "talk the talk" about social justice, they actually "walked the walk." They used their positions of power and their knowledge about the tenure and promotion process to ensure that we would become successful. When one of us (Thompson) left a teaching university to work at a research-based institution, Drew explained the importance of concentrating her efforts on writing and trying to get her work published. He read drafts of articles and book chapters, gave her feedback, and recommended journals to which she should submit her work. He also gave her good advice about dealing with the rejection that is inevitable in the publication process, and when the time came for her to go up for tenure, he prepared her tenure portfolio. Dr. Carol Franklin, a White woman supervisor, provided the other author (Louque) with similar advice and opportunities. Unfortunately, at other times— sometimes at the same institutions at which we had once had extremely supportive deans or chairs—we also ended up with unsupportive immediate supervisors.

The lessons we learned about the crucial role of strong and consistent support in increasing faculty satisfaction have been validated by research (Benjamin, 1997; Gregory, 1995; Hale, 2002; Irvine, 1992; Jackson, 2004; Jones, 2001; Louque, 1994; Turner & Myers, 2000). Although both male and female faculty need support in the work environment, for women (Gregory, 1995) and faculty of color (Turner & Myers, 2000), it is crucial. In "Don't Go It Alone," an essay that was published in the *Chronicle of Higher Education*, Ostrow (2002) described the experiences of women in the Academy. She said that in order to succeed, what women faculty most "need to avoid" is "isolation." According to Ostrow, "One of the most well-documented realities is the protective function of social support. People with strong personal connections fare better both physically and psychologically" (p. 2). Moreover, in spite of the competitive nature of higher education and its overemphasis on individualism, "We are more resilient, accomplish more, and feel more confident when we have close, supportive relationships," Ostrow stated (p. 2). One of the women who participated in Alfred's (2001) study of tenured Black female professors cited a supportive work environment as a main factor leading to success in the Academy for Black women. She stated, "I think the most important thing is to be at a school where you can work with the faculty, and especially to have someone who will support you" (p. 74).

In spite of the need for a supportive work environment, many faculty often find it lacking in the Academy (Gregory, 1995; Tierney & Rhoads, 1994; Turner & Myers, 2000; White & Siwatu, 2002). In a study involving a large sample of Black faculty in PWIs, Moore and Wagstaff (1974) found that all of the participants viewed themselves as "aliens" at their institutions. These feelings of isolation and alienation also plague many students of color (White & Siwatu, 2002). We have met numerous students of color, particularly females, who entered graduate school feeling very confident about their ability to succeed. Before long, however, the culture and climate of their postsecondary institution had caused them to go into "crisis mode." They began to question whether or not they were smart enough to earn the degrees they sought to attain. They also wondered whether or not they belonged in higher education. Some of these students prevailed in spite of their fears.

As we stated previously, research has shown that providing mentors is one of the best ways that postsecondary institutions can increase the likelihood that faculty and students of color will view institutions as supportive (Green, 2000; Gregory, 1995; Nelms, 2002; Rowley, 2000; Turner & Myers, 2000; Williams, 2001). Charlie Nelms, an African American male who has had a successful academic career as a professor and administrator, including a position as a vice president, said, "The common denominator for nearly every leader that I have known was the presence and active involvement of a mentor. As for me, my mentors have come in all sizes, ages, races, and genders; however, they were all committed to my success as a person, as a student, and as a leader" (2002, p. 192). According to Haynes-Burton (2004), individuals with mentors advance further, faster, and experience fewer adjustment problems than those without mentors. Dortch (2000) said, "Mentors are not social workers or surrogate parents or saviors. Mentors are advocates, advisers, and role models" (p. 7). Unfortunately, not all Black faculty members get the opportunity to have a mentor. In a study by Blackwell (1983), only one out of eight Black faculty said they had a mentor. According to Anderson, Frierson, and Lewis (1979), Black faculty "often obtain little professional or emotional support" (p. 66). Of course, the absence of genuine support and mentoring can result in a faculty member's failure to gain tenure and to be promoted, and even in a faculty member's decision to leave an institution.

In the introduction of this book and chapters 1 and 2, several issues that were related to the need for a supportive work environment surfaced. In this chapter, we present quantitative and qualitative results from our study that pertain specifically to support. We designed several questionnaire items to measure whether or not participants felt supported by Black and non-Black faculty and administrators at their current institution. Since marginalization is the opposite of a supportive environment, we also asked the participants about their related experiences with marginalization, undermining behavior, and professional jealousy (see table 3.1).

Support from Colleagues

Eighty-three percent of the survey respondents said that at their current institution, they had been supported by some African American

TABLE 3.1
Questionnaire Results Pertaining to Support

Questionnaire Item	% Who Agreed	% Who Disagreed
At my institution, some African American faculty have supported me.	83	11
At my institution, some African American administrators have supported me.	71	18
At my institution, some non-Black faculty have supported me.	88	8
At my institution, some non-Black administrators have supported me.	79	16
I have never felt that any of my colleagues were trying to undermine me at my current institution.	30	64
I have never felt that any administrator was trying to undermine me at my current institution.	38	58
At my institution, my professional success is important to my colleagues, chair, and dean.	60	33
I have been mentored by at least one other person.	71	29
I have never felt that I was marginalized in a department meeting.	28	57
I have never experienced any professional jealousy at work.	13	70

$N = 136$
Note: The difference in percentage totals that are less than 100 can be explained by the number of participants who failed to respond to certain statements.

faculty, but 11 percent disagreed. Regression analysis produced three predictors of how faculty responded to this survey item. The strongest predictor was whether or not the respondents believed that their professional success was important to their colleagues, department chair, and dean. Professors who said that their professional success was important to their colleagues and administrators were more likely to indicate that they had been supported by some Black faculty. The second strongest predictor was the respondents' rank. Senior faculty were more likely than junior faculty to say they had received support from some Black faculty. The third predictor was the number of Black faculty in the respondents' department. Surprisingly, this survey item was a negative predictor. In other words, having more Black colleagues increased the probability that respondents would state that they had not been supported by Black faculty.

Whereas 83 percent of the questionnaire respondents said they had been supported by some Black faculty, 88 percent said they had been supported by some non-Black faculty. Eight percent said they had not. Through regression analysis, we identified several predictors of how faculty responded to this survey item. As in the case of whether or not participants had been supported by some Black faculty, the strongest predictor of whether or not they stated that some non-Black faculty had supported them was the belief that their professional success was important to their colleagues and administrators. The second strongest predictor was believing that their experiences were valued by their colleagues and administrators. The third and fourth predictors also surfaced as predictors of whether or not participants had been supported by some Black faculty. As in the case of feeling supported by Black faculty, having more Black departmental colleagues increased the probability that respondents felt unsupported by non-Black faculty as well. Once again rank was also a predictive factor. The higher their rank, the more likely the respondents were to state that they had been supported by some of their non-Black colleagues. The last predictor pertained to racism. Participants who indicated they had experienced racism from a department chair or dean were less likely to say they had received support from some non-Black faculty.

Comments from faculty who participated in the interview phase of the study gave us more information about the quantitative results regarding support or a lack thereof from colleagues. For example, one professor said:

> My professional success is important to my colleagues. Some African American faculty have supported me. There is a woman, a full professor, who assisted me when I was going through my tenure review. She assisted me with writing a letter to the committee when they recommended against my tenure when I went up for early tenure. Other than that, there is no one there to mentor me, not at my college.
>
> Black Studies professors are now supporting me once I initiated contact, which I tried to do for years. But in the last year, I found tremendous support from the Black Studies Department, which is in a different college. Some non-Black administrators have supported me. My prior department chair was very supportive of me. I appreciate that support, especially during a time of controversy and the problem I was having.
>
> I have felt that one colleague is still determined to undermine me, especially when I was going through the tenure process, and I think she will do the same when I go for full professor. She happens to be Chair of the Tenure Review Committee. I'm certain that I will probably ask to be reviewed by someone else because I don't think I could trust her to be fair.

Support from Administrators

Seventy-one percent of the faculty stated that some African American administrators had supported them at their institution and 18 percent said they had not. Regression analysis produced one predictor of how faculty responded to this statement. Those who said their professional opinions were valued and respected at their institution were more likely to say they had been supported by some African American administrators.

Seventy-nine percent of the survey respondents said that some non-Black administrators had supported them at their institution but 16 percent disagreed. A regression equation produced two predictors of how faculty responded. The strongest predictor was feeling supported by some non-Black faculty. In other words, faculty who said they had been supported by some non-Black faculty were also likely to say they had been supported by some non-Black administrators. The second predictor pertained to cultural insensitivity. Faculty who said they had never experienced any cultural insensitivity from their department chair or dean were also likely to state they had received support from some non-Black administrators.

Feedback from the interviewees shed more light on the quantitative results. For instance, a professor in North Carolina said, "I've really been in an interesting situation, being at a relatively young university. We had a chancellor who was very supportive of diversity, even though I've had to come in and help define what diversity meant [despite the fact that it's] not something that would apply to me within my area."

Another professor expressed concern about whether or not her department chair would be supportive on a long-term basis. She explained:

> I don't think the new chair knows enough about my discipline to understand my work, nor has she taken the time. The dean came to my defense in a very profound way when I was up for tenure and wrote a letter to overturn the recommendation of a committee that did not recommend tenure. In that regard, I was surprised. My husband thinks she did it because she was afraid of his [my husband's] assertiveness. So, I don't think she really values what I know, the experiences I bring and the contribution I could make if I were given additional opportunities [like] some of my colleagues [have been given].

Other Types of Support

Two survey items gave the participants opportunities to describe whether or not they had received other types of support. Sixty percent of the respondents said at their institution their professional success was important to their colleagues, chair, and dean, but 33 percent disagreed. Faculty who had not experienced racism or cultural insensitivity and who were very satisfied at their institution were more likely to state that their professional success was important to their colleagues and administrators.

The second statement pertained to mentoring. Seventy-one percent of the faculty said they had been mentored by at least one person at their institution. Twenty-nine percent said they had not. Regression analysis revealed that three factors were the best predictors of their responses. The strongest predictor of having a mentor was working at an institution at which colleagues and administrators placed importance on the respondent's professional success. The second strongest predictor of being mentored was receiving support from some African American administrators. The third predictor was not having been undermined by any administrator at the respondent's current institution. Several interviewees provided more information about the importance of mentoring and working in a supportive environment. For example, one interviewee, who elaborated on the need for mentors and the importance of having a critical mass of Black faculty, explained:

> Number one, I think faculty that come in, especially faculty of color that come in without mentors or without prior experiences in higher education, really need a mentor. It doesn't matter if it's the same race; they need a mentor. This college needs to actively work to bring faculty, males of color, and more females, to balance hiring practices because I think when Blacks have a more visible presence, there will be the respect that will be accorded to the groups, such as it is to the Latinos now that they have a critical mass. They are a sizeable force. So, I think the numbers are important. There has to

be a critical mass of African American scholars so the students can respect them and see them as someone of worth.

This interviewee also said:

I think it is important to attach African Americans to large grants that have longevity. We are typically called on to the hot spots and called on to do work in troubled urban schools, but we don't get multiyear grants. You have a one time shot where you work your chin off and then you have to hustle to try to find money. We're not given opportunities for appointments outside the classroom as frequently and with the same proportional frequency as other colleagues are, so that we don't gain other experiences in the Academy other than community service. I have a bit of experience working with community service. We need opportunities to get appointments that will enrich our backgrounds, so that when we go up for reviews, committees may not know us and will look at us as people who contribute, and not as just peripheral faculty members. Sometimes, I think we get marginalized because we're underrepresented and so I think that is important. We have to network not just with Blacks, but with other Whites who could help our community.

The Opposite of Support: Marginalization, Professional Jealousy, and Undermining Behavior

As director of secondary education at a PWI where she used to work, one of us authors once scheduled a meeting with program faculty and the program assistant. However, unbeknownst to the author, a White female lecturer told the secretary to cancel the meeting because she was not going to be able to attend it. Thereafter, the secretary put memos stating that the meeting would be postponed in everyone's mailbox but the author's. On the original date that the meeting was scheduled to be held, the author arrived on campus for the meeting. Before going to the room where the meeting was to be held, she went to the main office to pick up her materials for the meeting. After chatting with her for a while the secretary said she hadn't expected to see her on campus that day since the meeting had been postponed. The surprised author asked the secretary why the meeting had been re-scheduled. When the author found out what had happened, she questioned the program assistant and the secretary to find out why they had followed the instructions of a lecturer instead of the director. They had no response.

This is an example of one type of behavior in higher education that can cause Black faculty, as well as non-Black faculty with similar experiences, to believe that certain individuals in the workplace may not have their best interest at heart and that they may actually be resorting to subterfuge that could harm their career. In this case, the author did not know for certain if the secretary had merely forgotten to notify her of the decision to postpone the meeting, or had deliberately chosen not to inform her. What she did know for certain was that both the secretary and lecturer had overstepped their bounds and made a decision that they had no authority to make. Therefore, the author concluded that both had engaged in undermining behavior. William Watkins (2002) wrote boldly about the many guises of unprofessional behavior in the Academy that faculty sometimes face when he said, "The new Black professor is suspect. Is s(h)e really a scholar or did the department need a minority? . . . The false face is soon stripped away as those White and white-haired professors who appear so intelligent and worldly, lapse into guttersnipping, backstabbing, and murdermouthing in polysyllabic prose" (p. 101).

Like undermining behavior, marginalization is another reason why faculty may perceive postsecondary institutions to be unsupportive places (Smith, 1995; Turner & Myers, 2000; W. Watkins, 2002). According to Lipman-Blumen (2005), "There are many grounds on which one can feel isolated and alienated, beginning with differences based on gender, education, ethnicity, age, religion, and so on" (p. 41). Turner and Myers (2000) found that "faculty of color find themselves outside the informal networks of the department" (p. 24). Williams (2001) said the "severe marginalization" that some faculty of color experience has been attributed to several factors: "poor institutional fit, cross cultural and social differences, lack of support, . . . feelings of isolation, experiences with prejudice and discrimination, lower salaries, low professional ranks, and lack of tenured status" (p. 93).

As we stated previously, we have noticed that our voices are often ignored when decisions are being made in various meetings—even when these decisions will have an impact on us as professors and also have an impact on our students. This subtle form of marginalization has led us to believe that some PWIs are guilty of tokenism (Turner & Myers, 2000). They may hire Black professors but may only do so for "window-dressing" purposes. In other words, they never really expect or will permit them to become fully included members of the faculty (Turner & Myers, 2000). A positive socialization experience has been linked to faculty satisfaction, productivity, and effectiveness (Van Maanen & Schein, 1979). For faculty of color who decide to remain, intellectual challenge, freedom to pursue research interests, and the opportunity to promote racial and ethnic understanding are among the factors that keep them in the Academy (Turner, 2002). Conversely, faculty who perceive their socialization experiences as negative may experience stress and anxiety. Therefore, a faculty member who is dissatisfied, unproductive, and ineffective is more likely to leave an institution of higher education permanently.

We have also noticed that another subtle manifestation of non-support often stems from professional jealousy. The result is that highly productive Black and non-Black faculty may become the objects of snide remarks and criticism by less productive colleagues. In worst-case scenarios, as we noted previously, jealous colleagues can undermine productive scholars by discouraging students from taking their classes and discouraging students from inviting them to serve on dissertation and other committees. Then, such colleagues can always say, "She may do a lot of research and writing, but she doesn't have a good reputation with students." These comments can be used against the productive faculty member when tenure and promotion decisions are being made. In the following sections, we present the results of our study pertaining to marginalization in department meetings, professional jealousy, and undermining behavior, in order to illustrate how these factors can create a non-supportive work environment that might create dissatisfaction among Black faculty and even compel some to leave their institution.

Marginalization

Twenty-eight percent of the questionnaire respondents said they had never felt marginalized in department meetings, but nearly 60 percent said they had. Of these respondents, 24 percent said the marginalization occurred rarely, but 32 percent said it happened more frequently. Nearly 90 percent of the respondents who felt marginalized in department meetings said that this marginalization had a moderate to strong effect on them. Twelve percent said this problem might actually prompt them to leave their institution. Bivariate correlation analysis showed us that faculty who felt marginalized in department meetings also had experienced racism and cultural insensitivity at their institution, and worked at institutions where racism and cultural insensitivity were common.

Professional Jealousy

Thirteen percent of the questionnaire respondents said they had never experienced any professional jealousy at work. Seventy percent said they had. Although 20 percent said that it occurred rarely, 50 percent said it occurred more frequently. Nearly 70 percent of the participants who had experienced professional jealousy said it had a moderate to strong effect on them. The main factors that differentiated this group of faculty from those who said they had never experienced any professional jealousy were that they worked at institutions where racism and cultural insensitivity were common and had affected them personally, and they tended to be dissatisfied with how their immediate supervisor had handled racist or culturally insensitive situations that affected the respondents personally.

Undermining Behavior

Two questionnaire items gave participants opportunities to state whether or not they had ever felt they were being undermined at their current institution by their colleagues or administrators. Only 30 percent of the faculty said they had never felt that any of their colleagues were trying to undermine them. However, 64 percent disagreed. A regression equation produced three predictors. Faculty who were most likely to say they had never felt undermined by a colleague were also likely to state they had never experienced racism from a department chair or dean at their current institution. Second, they believed their knowledge about their race and culture was valued by their colleagues, chair, and dean. Finally, they said they had never experienced racism from any (non-chair or non-dean) administrator.

Regarding undermining behavior from administrators, only 38 percent of the faculty said they had never felt that any administrator was trying to undermine them at their current institution. Nearly 60 percent disagreed. Regression analysis produced four predictors of how faculty responded. First, faculty who stated they had never felt undermined by colleagues at their current institution also tended to say the same about administrators. Second, respondents who had never experienced cultural insensitivity from any university administrator also said they had not been undermined by administrators. Third, faculty who believed their contributions were valued by their colleagues and administrators were unlikely to have ever felt undermined by administrators. The last predictor was negative. Faculty who said they had never felt undermined by any administrator at their current institution were also likely to indicate they had not received support from any African American faculty at their current institution.

Several interviewees described their thoughts and experiences related to undermining behavior. For example, one professor said:

> I've never felt that I have ever had an administrator try to undermine me, but I have felt that I couldn't count on support, which is common. . . . Certain African American faculty are less respected

than other faculty. We just don't have enough members to assess whether it is because we are African American. We are certainly not a premium there. Our research is less respected. . . . African American faculty who speak out about racism are labeled "troublemakers." I think I'm not labeled a "troublemaker" as much as I am [labeled] one who you might want to avoid. So, that may be to say, "Tenure can be denied by faculty."

Summary

Three main themes emerged from the results that we presented in this chapter. First, the overwhelming majority of the participants in our study felt supported by their colleagues and administrators at their current institution. The fact that higher percentages of participants said they received support from non-Black faculty and non-Black administrators than from Blacks can be explained in at least two ways. The most obvious is that they worked at institutions at which they found non-Blacks to be more supportive.

The second possibility is that respondents who said they had not been supported by Black faculty and/or Black administrators may have taught at institutions at which Black faculty and administrators were nonexistent or so extremely underrepresented that they had limited contact with each other. However, the fact that there was an inverse relationship between the number of Black faculty the respondents had in their department and saying they had not felt supported by other Black faculty refutes this explanation. Because there was also an inverse relationship between the number of Black colleagues respondents had in their department and not feeling supported by non-Black faculty either, it is possible that in some departments and institutions Black faculty feel just as isolated and alienated from each other as they do from non-Blacks (Silver et al., 1988).

Nearly seventy years ago, Harlem Renaissance writer Zora Neale Hurston, who taught at at least two postsecondary institutions during her lifetime, bemoaned the fact that some African Americans spent more effort "to keep somebody else from getting somewhere than . . . to get somewhere [themselves]" (Kaplan, 2002, p. 386). In a specific example of the predilection of some Blacks to not only be non-supportive of other Blacks in the Academy, but to actually attempt to undermine them, Hurston described a situation that occurred at an HBCU. The efforts of the culprits included dissuading students from taking a certain African American professor's courses in order "to make him so unpopular that he must leave" (Kaplan, 2002, p. 387). The victim of these machinations was none other than James Weldon Johnson, one of the most outstanding Black scholars in U.S. history and the author of the "Negro National Anthem."

In another example, Hurston wrote a letter in 1937, while working at an HBCU. In the letter, Hurston criticized a prominent Black college administrator for refusing to help a young Black artist get established professionally. "She snubbed him terribly and almost quit speaking to me," Hurston wrote. "Afraid attention would be directed away from herself. The heifer! The crusher of talent" (Kaplan, 2002, p. 405). Hurston's letters also contain many examples of times when she personally felt the sting and painful consequences of undermining behavior from other African Americans, which some of her supporters believe resulted in the ruination of her literary career.

Unfortunately, like Hurston, we authors have also seen instances or heard about cases when Black faculty and administrators were unsupportive of other Black faculty. Furthermore, we have felt a similar sting from some African American senior professors and administrators who were in a position to be helpful to junior faculty but chose not to, and from those who chose to snub junior faculty and who refused to "step up to the plate" and serve as mentors, not only to faculty but to Black students as well. Moreover, as we noted in the introduction, at least one of us experienced undermining behavior from a Black administrator at a PWI who routinely targeted junior faculty and women and attempted to turn them against each other.

It is difficult enough for Black faculty to deal with racism, cultural insensitivity, marginalization, unfair evaluations, isolation, and so many other problems that permeate many postsecondary institutions, but when non-support from other Black faculty is added to the list, the work environment can seem even more unbearable. One reason for this behavior might be that some Black faculty are so busy trying to survive the politics and pressures of the Academy that they themselves have little energy, time, or even expertise that they feel will benefit others. Another reason why the participants in our study were more likely to say they had not been supported by other Black faculty might be that they worked in departments where their Black colleagues were untenured junior professors who were "learning the ropes" and trying to navigate their way through the confusing and contradictory labyrinth of the Academy themselves. In other words, they may have felt that they had little to give to a colleague who was in need of support. Regardless of the reason, the findings make it clear that Black faculty must rely on the support of non-Blacks, the dominant group in PWIs. Moreover, faculty and administrators must strive not to pit Black faculty against each other but encourage collaboration and collegiality. One of the clearest messages that emanated from the data that we presented in this chapter is that many of the study's participants believed that they would be happier if there were a critical mass of Black faculty in their department and institution. Additionally, the majority of participants, 83 percent, said they had been supported by some Black faculty and 71 percent said that Black administrators had supported them. Like many of the participants in our study, many researchers have emphasized the importance of having a critical mass of Blacks in postsecondary institutions (Gregory, 1995; Smith, 1995; Turner & Myers, 2000; White & Siwatu, 2002).

Other findings indicated that the majority of participants in our study said that at one time or another, they had felt that one or more colleagues and administrators at their institution had tried to undermine them, had marginalized them, or subjected them to professional jealousy. These results speak volumes about the climate of many institutions and may be among the reasons why postsecondary institutions can be perceived as toxic places. In our opinion, it is unlikely for an institution to be a supportive place where faculty can thrive when undermining behavior, marginalization, and professional jealousy are rampant. For Black faculty—members of a historically oppressed group—it is sometimes difficult to know when what appears to be undermining behavior is truly based on an innocent mistake or when it is done deliberately or is even racially motivated. As Turner and Myers (2000) maintained, "To achieve campus cultures that are truly inclusive, institutions must emphasize cooperation, and community" (p. 221).

An additional finding revealed that although most participants felt supported at their institution, many faculty did not. Many said they had not been mentored and that their professional success was not important to their colleagues, department chair, or dean. Like other researchers who have examined ways in which the Academy can increase Black faculty satisfaction and, consequently, retention rates, we underscore the need for strong and consistent support in the workplace. This support must include a work environment in which the professional opinions of Black faculty are respected, collaboration is encouraged, and the professional success of Black faculty is important to their colleagues, chair, dean, and other administrators—points that we made in the previous chapter. Moreover, as we noted at the beginning of this chapter, mentoring is a crucial factor in the professional success of women faculty and faculty of color (Garcia, 2000; Jackson, 2004; Louque, 1994; Turner, 2002). In spite of this, many Black faculty are not assigned formal mentors. Nearly 30 percent of the participants in our study said they were not mentored at all. In a study conducted by Jackson, all of the faculty recognized the importance of mentoring. However, although the majority of the Black and Hispanic faculty said they mentored other faculty, only a small percentage said that they themselves had mentors.

In conclusion, one way that the Academy can increase Black faculty satisfaction is to ensure that when they are hired all faculty members participate in a formal mentoring program consisting of qualified and willing mentors (Gregory, 1995; Hale, 2002; Quezada & Louque, 2004; Turner & Myers, 2000). According to Ostrow (2002), good mentors possess several characteristics and display specific behaviors. They "promote [the mentee's] professional productivity, foster confidence in [the mentee's] abilities, and help [the mentee] build enthusiasm in [his or her] field" (p. 4). In short, the mentor–mentee "relationship should be a source of acceptance and personal support, as well as information about how to be successful. Particularly for new female faculty members, an effective mentor is sensitive to, and supportive of [the mentee's] non-work responsibilities" (p. 4). Obviously, it also goes without saying, that an effective mentor must be willing to serve as a mentor. Dortch stated, "All that's required is a commitment to make a difference, a willingness to listen and hear, and the discipline to balance your heart and mind" (2000, p. 7). According to Toth (2002b), "It is much better to have faculty volunteers . . . assigned to mentees—for when mentoring is formal and institutional, it's not seen as a quirk of personality or misread as some kind of stalking" (p. 3).

In "Coming to Terms with Being a Young, Black Female Academic in U.S. Higher Education," Williams (2001) wrote about the importance of being mentored and also of serving as a mentor and role model. She said:

> I truly believe that I have made a difference in the lives of the individuals I have taught and worked with in the Academy. Yet, I also know that these same students and colleagues have made a difference in my life as well. Through my experiences in higher education, I have learned the importance of survival by bridging alliances with others across race, class, gender, religion, abilities, sexuality, and age. (p. 101)

In our own cases, the men, Dr. David E. Drew and Dr. Randall Lindsey, who chose to mentor us, possessed all of the characteristics of good mentors. They volunteered to do so, took their mentoring duties seriously, were sensitive to our unique experiences as African American women at PWIs, were patient, gave good advice, applauded our successes, honored our voices, taught us some important unwritten "rules," and helped us to "reframe" various incidents. These actions provided us with much-needed support during numerous difficult periods. In the next chapter, we discuss the unwritten "rules" of the Academy, a topic that expands on the importance of a supportive work environment for Black faculty, and underscores the message that good mentoring can make a positive difference.

4

DID THIS PACKAGE COME WITH INSTRUCTIONS?

How the Unwritten "Rules" of the Academy Can Affect Black Faculty

I N *Black Children: Their Roots, Culture and Learning Styles* (1986), Janice Hale-Benson, an African American professor at Wayne State University, said that for many African American children, going to school is like traveling to a foreign land. The theoretical underpinning of Hale-Benson's statement—the theory of cultural discontinuity— maintains that African American students' underachievement may be caused by a mismatch between their home culture and the culture of the school (Au, 1993; Ladson-Billings, 2001). School culture, which is based on White middle-class norms, is extremely different from the home culture of African American students from rural and urban communities (Thompson, 2002, 2004b).

Higher education is no different. In her "Ms. Mentor" advice column that is published regularly in the *Chronicle of Higher Education*'s Career Network section, Emily Toth underscored this point when addressing a complaint from a White professor. The professor had complained about the behavior of an African American colleague whom he had offered to mentor. Toth advised him to think of the woman "as a foreigner in the land where you've been comfortably ensconced all your life" (2002b, p. 2). She also told him, "African American faculty members find themselves patronized or bullied, but few are mentored about hidden agendas and processes" (p. 2). Furthermore, according to William Watkins (2002), "The Black professor must find out what the university culture is about and how to negotiate a sometimes hostile system" (p. 101). Thus, for many African American faculty and students—especially those who are first-generation college graduates—the Academy is similar to a foreign land (Jarmon, 2001; Woods, 2001).

As African Americans, we, the authors, have found that the gulf between our background experiences, beliefs, and behaviors, and the climate, common practices, and unwritten rules of the Academy is wide. Often, some of these unwritten rules have dumbfounded us. The main reason was that we were not fully prepared for the politics, covert racism, superiority complexes, ethnocentricism, "culture of arrogance" (which we will discuss in chapter 7 and in the conclusion)— and sometimes, just plain nutty behavior—that permeates the institutional climate of some of the PWIs at which we have taught. This could stem from the fact that both of us were socialized and grew up in predominantly Black environments, and we are first-generation college graduates. Perhaps African Americans who are socialized in predominantly White environments are better prepared to handle these problems.

All we know is that in certain situations, we were often at a loss as to how to proceed. In other words, we were not only ignorant of the unwritten rules of these institutions, but when we learned them— usually from our mentors or the hard way—we had to figure out the appropriate strategies to use. On top of this, we learned that the unwritten rules can vary from institution to institution. Moreover, unwritten rules exist at both PWIs and HBCUs.

An article in the *Chronicle of Higher Education* illustrated this fact. In "AAUP Censures a College, Criticizes Another, and Drops 3 from List," Fogg (2004b) described a case involving Philander Smith College, an HBCU. According to Fogg, a Black assistant professor at Philander Smith accused the university of violating her right to free speech "when it dismissed her on the grounds of insubordination" (p.

A21). The professor "was terminated after speaking to a local newspaper about conditions at the college without first alerting the president's office" (p. A21). Moreover, Fogg stated that the college also fired four other professors. After an investigation, the American Association of University Professors (AAUP) sided with all of the fired professors and opted to censure Philander Smith. In the aftermath, the assistant professor who had accused the college of violating her right to free speech continued to maintain that her rights had been violated. On the other hand, college representatives disagreed and argued emphatically that she had "violated a simple policy that appeared in a memorandum on public statements sent out by the college president" (p. A21). Although numerous faculty sided with the president's office, at the time when the official AAUP censure became public, the assistant professor was planning to sue the college (Fogg, 2004b).

Regardless of whether or not the assistant professor and other faculty were familiar with the college's policy ahead of time, the controversy illustrates the fact that unwritten rules and expectations exist in the Academy that may or may not be as explicit or as well known as they should be (Alfred, 2001; Jarmon, 2001). These rules pertain to many aspects of higher education, including acceptable behavior for faculty, the value placed on the types of work that faculty do, the tenure process, and the value that is placed on various types of research (Jarmon, 2001; Smith, 1995; Turner & Myers, 2000; W. Watkins, 2002; White & Siwatu, 2002). As in the Philander Smith case, some of these rules only surface under a cloud of controversy. Others surface in articles or essays about the Academy that were written by individuals who learned the unwritten or little-known rules the hard way, like we often did.

For instance, the *Chronicle of Higher Education*'s Career Network segment describes some of these rules periodically. One example is an essay, "Institutions Are Not Your Friends" (2001), that James M. Jasper wrote. In this essay, Jasper debunked several myths about postsecondary institutions and revealed some of the unwritten or lesser known rules. Although the Academy is highly respected, he said, this aura of respectability can obscure the realities. According to Jasper, not only are postsecondary institutions bureaucratic, self-serving organizations, but since "some administrators have emerged from academic ranks . . . it is possible to think they are just like the rest of us. But they no longer are" (p. 1). Moreover, "Institutions serve all sorts of important social functions but protecting individual employees is not one of them" (p. 2). A third unwritten rule, which Jasper learned after being denied tenure at New York University (NYU), is that even when tenure denials are found to be unwarranted, universities are unlikely to overturn them. As a result of his own experiences at NYU, Jasper concluded, "our institution is not concerned with distinguishing the truth . . . it wants to protect itself. In many cases it is not even possible to discover how it made its decisions, meaning there is no opportunity for rebuttal" (p. 2).

As in the previous example, several of the unwritten or lesser known rules of the Academy pertain to the tenure process. For example, in "Academic Revenge," Toth (2002a) illustrated one of these rules as she responded to a question from a professor who was denied tenure. According to the professor, the denial stemmed from "two damning letters from outside reviewers," including one reviewer whom she had considered to be her friend (p. 1). In responding to this disappointed professor, Toth revealed two of the lesser known rules of higher education. One rule or common practice that Toth described clearly illustrates why the politics in postsecondary institutions can be pernicious and why undermining behavior—a topic that we discussed in the previous chapter—is rampant. According to Toth, "Experienced academics know that most good deeds can double as revenge scenarios. You may, for instance, nominate your enemies for useless honors. Get them appointed to countless busy-but-powerless committees. Drown them in paperwork, while praising them for 'service.' Pass none of the reforms they suggest, and use their vitas for paper airplanes. Shred their documents. Lose their memos" (p. 2). A second and more important unwritten rule is, "In tenure decisions, letters are often read carefully for positive or negative nuances—depending on whether [the individual's] colleagues really want to keep her," according to Toth (2002a, p. 2).

There are at least three other unwritten rules about the tenure process: tenure practices can vary among institutions (Fogg, 2004a), tenure decisions can be based on arbitrary and questionable practices (Bell, 1994; Gregory, 1995), and the tenure process is designed to weed out nonconformists. As White observed, "One way they can punish you is by not giving you tenure" (White & Siwatu, 2002, p. 84). In "Hello . . . I Must Be Going," an article that was published in the *Chronicle of Higher Education*, Fogg (2004a) described common practices at Ivy League institutions. At Ivy League colleges and universities, tenure practices are not uniform, according to Fogg. In fact, Harvard University, Yale University, and Columbia University have no formal tenure tracks, and the length of time that untenured professors can work at these universities varies depending on the university. Conversely, Princeton University, Brown University, Cornell University, Dartmouth College, and the University of Pennsylvania have formal tenure tracks, and untenured professors can usually work at these institutions about six years before going up for tenure (Fogg, 2004a).

Recently, some Ivy League institutions have been criticized for their tenure practices that result in a high number of junior professors being forced to leave after a tenure denial. Some critics have accused these institutions, particularly Harvard, Princeton, and Yale, of giving mixed messages to junior faculty, and holding to a time-honored tradition of bringing in faculty who have earned tenure elsewhere at the expense of untenured professors (Fogg, 2004a). In spite of this longstanding tradition, some junior faculty said they had naively assumed that they would be treated differently. One of these critics, an assistant professor who had taught at Harvard for nine years, "had published 31 articles and three books, and had four more books accepted for publication" was not even "formally considered" when a tenure slot became available (Fogg, 2004b, p. A10). As a result of widespread criticism, Harvard, Yale, Princeton, and Columbia are either in the process of reviewing their tenure practices or have already implemented reforms (Fogg, 2004a).

Finally, another unwritten rule related to the tenure process is that the entire procedure is designed to weed out "radicals" before they gain tenure, and to create "conformists." William Watkins (2002) said, "Tenure is at the heart of the socialization process. It enforces conformity, discipline, and most importantly, it influences ideology as the new professor must enter the strange and vexing world of publishing" (p. 103). In *A Tenured Professor* (1990), a novel about the Academy, John Kenneth Galbraith revealed this rule via a dialogue between a senior professor and a junior professor who wanted to help the "economically disadvantaged" through his research agenda. The senior professor told him that his research agenda was unwise and he would not get tenured. When the junior professor asked for an explanation, he replied:

> Tenure was originally invented to protect radical professors, those who challenged the accepted order. But we don't have such people anymore at the universities, and the reason *is* tenure. When the time comes to grant it nowadays, the radicals get screened out. That's its principal function. (p. 38)

When the junior professor asked, "Suppose one waits until one has tenure to show one's liberal tendencies?" the senior professor replied, "By then conformity will be a habit. You'll no longer be a threat to the peace and comfort of our ivied walls. The system really works" (p. 39).

Bell (1994) made a related point by stating that during the hiring and promotion process, faculty are "enormously effective in using the tenure system to exclude those who, despite impressive credentials, are deemed unacceptable because of ideology, personality differences, and even more arbitrary reasons" (p. 75). Moreover, according to Bell "otherwise honorable faculty members engage in the most unscrupulous, underhanded conduct to avoid hiring or promoting individuals they did not wish to see admitted to their ranks. They have lied, maligned character, altered rules, manufactured precedents, and distorted policies" (p. 75). Some of these same issues surfaced in *Clark v. Claremont University*. In this case, an African American professor said that he was denied tenure as a result of racial discrimination. In the end, a court ruled in his favor (Baez & Centra, 1995).

For Black faculty, knowing the requirements for tenure and the existing unwritten "rules" is crucial to their success in the Academy. In "Unwritten Rules of the Game," Jarmon (2001), a Black woman, wrote about her experiences as a Black female junior faculty who did not know the unwritten rules of postsecondary institutions. She said, "I knew very little about the Academy and the 'politics' involved. Therefore, my previous experiences [as a graduate student and adjunct instructor at the same university where she was hired on a tenure track] could not adequately inform me of my new role" (p. 176). Jarmon added, "I cannot recall a single incident where someone offered to 'formally' mentor me as a junior faculty member, so I had to find alternative strategies to figure out how things worked" (p. 176). Fortunately for Jarmon, the department secretary was able to assist her.

Furthermore, ignorance of the unwritten rules regarding the tenure process have long been cited as a factor affecting Black faculty satisfaction and retention. Many years ago, S. V. Brown (1988) found that Blacks have had the lowest faculty progression and retention rates in higher education and that they were promoted and tenured at lower rates than any other group. This report also indicated that Blacks were beginning to avoid selecting careers in the Academy. Given the existence of so many unwritten rules about tenure, it is little wonder that William Watkins (2002) said, "Nothing is more intimidating to the Black male professor than the tenure process" (p. 103).

Some of the unwritten rules that are often detrimental to Black faculty also pertain to the value placed on getting published versus engaging in community service (Jarmon, 2001). Blacks continually have to fight for understanding and acceptance of their work (Alfred, 2001; Turner & Myers, 2000; W. Watkins, 2002; White & Siwatu,

2002; Woods, 2001). Antonio's (2002) study of faculty of color indicated that on the surface, White faculty have produced more research (journal articles and books), but faculty of color spend more time conducting research. Faculty of color also place a high degree of importance on their research activities. Furthermore, Antonio concluded that faculty of color were a third more likely to be involved with student groups involved in community service and 29 percent more likely to be involved with community service. Overall, the study demonstrated that faculty of color had a high commitment to research activities and were more explicit about connecting their academic work to their service to the non-university communities around them. However, Jarmon (2001) said, "It is critical for junior faculty, especially faculty of color, to find balance between their commitments and interests in the community (within and beyond the university) and the demands of scholarship and research. Community service is important, but as a junior scholar it is imperative to weigh it according to the type of institution where one is employed" (p. 179). She added, "At major research universities, community service takes a minor role because establishing a research agenda and publication record is paramount" (p. 179). In an effort to offset time management problems that can result in a lack of time for writing and conducting research, White urged Black junior faculty to request release time and a reduced teaching load in order to have more time for their research (White & Siwatu, 2002). Gregory (1995) made a similar point.

Two other unwritten rules pertain to research. It is a well-known but usually unwritten rule in the Academy that when African Americans carve out a research agenda that focuses primarily on "black" issues, their non-Black colleagues are likely to disparage their work (Smith, 1995; Turner & Myers, 2000; W. Watkins, 2002; White & Siwatu, 2002). Conversely, when non-Blacks, particularly Whites, devote their research to diversity, multiculturalism, and "black" issues, they are treated more respectfully by White academics. Perna (2002) noted that a related issue is even more pertinent, and that is whether or not African Americans should focus on race in their research at all.

In a book review, Perna reported that African Americans should consider conducting "research that is respected by peers" (p. 242) in order to attain tenure and promotion, and because there is a perception in the Academy that research centered around race or the study of African Americans is devalued. Astin, Antonio, Cress, and Astin (1997) said that seeing their work devalued is a common form of discrimination that faculty of color experience in the Academy.

Another unwritten rule that has a direct impact on Black faculty is "Individual achievement is valued above all else. Competition is fierce" (Ostrow, 2002, p. 1), and we (the authors) would even say it is ruthless. In contrast, according to Toth, "Black faculty members at most universities also try to 'give back to the community'—give time and money to each other, to students, to troubled children" and this "does clash with the career-at-all-costs mentality that makes ambitious people 'successful'" (2002b, p. 2).

A second unwritten rule pertaining to research stems from the quantitative versus qualitative research debate. In recent decades, qualitative research has emerged as a respectable form of scholarship. Many graduate students have produced exemplary dissertations that are based on observations, interviews, case studies, focus group feedback, and other forms of qualitative research or by using mixed methods that they later converted into reader-friendly books. Some of these books have made important contributions to the existing body of research. Among these dissertations that became reader-friendly books are Laurie Olsen's *Made in America: Immigrant Students in Our Public Schools* (1997); Fordham's *Blacked Out: Dilemmas of Race, Identity, and Success at Capital High* (1996); and Ferguson's *Bad Boys: Public Schools in the Making of Black Masculinity* (2001). Despite the great strides that qualitative researchers have made in bringing respectability to this genre of scholarship, the fact remains that there is still an unwritten rule in the Academy that results in more prestige being given to quantitative research.

Smith (1995) referred to the ongoing controversy regarding the value that is placed on certain types of scholarship as the debate over "inclusive theory" and "inclusive scholarship." She explained, "Part of the intensity of the current discussion about diversity reflects the 'contested terrain' of who gets to define and who gets to name the questions and methods of our research" (p. 236). However, she underscored the fact that true inclusiveness can only occur when the scholarly contributions and voices of historically marginalized groups are valued by the Academy.

The fact that certain members of the Academy tend to disparage the research of Black faculty when they focus on "black issues," and that many Black faculty prefer qualitative research over quantitative research can be extremely problematic for Black faculty and students. Many elect to become academics primarily because they want to conduct research that can improve the plight of the masses of African Americans, a topic that we will return to later in this book. Moreover, there is a long and rich history among educated Blacks of conducting this type of research. For example, in addition to writing short stories and novels, Zora Neale Hurston, a trained anthropologist, was one of the first African American women to conduct ethnographic research. At the time when she traveled throughout the United States and even abroad collecting her data, her work was often ridiculed and widely criticized—even by other Blacks (Kaplan, 2002). Today, more than a half century later, other Black researchers find themselves in a similar predicament.

Although many African American faculty may be as ignorant of the unwritten rules of the Academy (Jarmon, 2001) as we (the authors) were until we learned many of them through the school of hard knocks and advice from our mentors, these rules can have a huge impact on their success or lack of success in higher education. Research has indicated that any new faculty member—not just African Americans—may struggle to understand the culture of the institution, feel lonely and isolated, and lack collegial support (Johnson & Harvey, 2002), but not knowing the rules can be detrimental (Alfred, 2001; Jarmon, 2001). Fortunately, like others who have written about this topic, Bowser, Auletta, and Jones (1999) have removed the shroud of secrecy about some of the unwritten rules that many new faculty may not know. These authors identified six of the most important unwritten rules and realities, including several that we have already described in this chapter that faculty need to know:

1. The university is political.
2. Personal and professional networks are powerful forces.
3. People of color are perceived as threats.
4. Hidden agendas vary in sophistication.
5. Hidden agendas cannot tolerate public exposure.
6. Perceptions matter.

In "Unwritten Rules of the Game," Jarmon (2001) spoke candidly about several facts that Black faculty should know in order to be successful in the Academy. She emphasized the importance of publishing in the "right" type of journals, knowing how to prepare a portfolio for tenure and promotion, devoting enough time to writing for publication, honing one's teaching skills, networking, and collaborating with senior faculty on publications. Alfred (2001) said that as a result of mentoring, the tenured Black women whom she studied already were aware of the rules when they became junior professors, and "Although they found some of the rules inappropriate, they chose to follow the rules to ensure their success in the culture" (p. 67). One of the participants in Alfred's study mentioned two rules that we have not previously mentioned that are important for Black faculty to know: "You need to be visible in the community that you say you are an expert in" and "You need to be visible at your national conferences and [in publications in your field]" (pp. 71–72).

In our opinion, to a large extent, the unwritten rules of the Academy continue to control the degree to which faculty of color and women participate in higher education. These unwritten rules are perpetuated because the historical privilege of White Americans often goes unexamined (Akbar, 2002; Hilliard, 2002; W. Watkins, 2002), and students of color and faculty of color are still perceived by some as "other" and are treated as outsiders (Turner & Myers, 2000; West, 2002). For example, Jarmon (2001) recounted that as a junior faculty member, she tried to be friendly, collegial, and a good citizen at her university. However, when she "asked [her] colleagues questions . . . sometimes [she] got answers and other times [she] did not" (p. 176). Consequently, Jarmon "felt a sense of isolation" (p. 176). She admitted, "I wondered how I would ever become a part of their world. I often questioned why I was at this research institution when my heart and soul were into teaching and community service" (pp. 176–177).

We wanted to learn more about these rules and their impact on Black faculty. Therefore, in the remainder of this chapter we present the results of our study pertaining to Black faculty's beliefs and experiences with the unwritten rules and common practices at their institution. As we noted previously, we have learned that not only are some of the rules inexplicit and confusing, but they can vary from institution to institution. For example, at the first PWI at which one of us started out on a tenure track, the author was told by a department chair to "keep your mouth shut in meetings until you're tenured, because nobody wants to hear what you have to say anyway, and it can hurt you when you go up for tenure." At the second PWI where this author worked in a tenure-track position, the meeting protocol was shared with her implicitly. Instead of telling her to be quiet during meetings, her department chair would frown or make disparaging remarks when she spoke. At the author's third position as a tenure-track professor at a PWI, instead of waiting for the rule to be explained explicitly, or to infer it through implicit behavior, she became proactive: When she was hired, she asked her mentor, who was also the dean, whether or not junior faculty were expected to be quiet during meetings. To her relief, he said, "No. We want to hear your ideas and to get to know you better." However, over time, he also emphasized the importance of picking and choosing one's battles wisely, and avoiding the politics as much as possible until she had gained tenure.

In order to give Black faculty an opportunity to identify unwritten rules and common practices, we included the statement, "In your opinion, which of the following practices or beliefs are unwritten 'rules' or common practices at your institution?" on the questionnaire. Five related statements followed. Respondents could select some, all, or none of the options. The second component of this questionnaire item asked, "Which of the aforementioned unwritten 'rules' or practices at your institution have been most upsetting or problematic for you?" Respondents could select some, all, or none of the related statements (see table 4.1).

Results

The first related questionnaire item said, "There is a 'pecking order' in which junior faculty are treated less respectfully than senior faculty." Fifty-nine percent of the respondents agreed with this statement and 32 percent said it had been problematic for them. An in-depth look at pertinent descriptive statistics gave us more information about the participants who said the pecking order existed at their institution. A lower percentage of these individuals indicated that they were very satisfied at their institution when compared to the percentage of respondents in the total sample who were. Moreover, a smaller percentage of the faculty who said there was a pecking order at their institution were tenured than in the general sample of participants. Finally, a slightly higher percentage of these respondents tended to be the only Black faculty member in their department in comparison to the percentage in the total sample.

A second survey item said, "Community service is less respected than research and publishing." Sixty-four percent of the faculty agreed and 36 percent said that it was an unwritten rule at their institution that had affected them personally.

A third survey item stated, "African American faculty who speak out about racism and cultural insensitivity in the Academy are labeled as 'troublemakers.'" Fifty percent of the survey respondents agreed and 43 percent said that this unwritten rule or common practice had been personally upsetting or problematic for them. When we exam-

TABLE 4.1
Percentage of Participants Who Agreed or Disagreed That Various Unwritten
"Rules" and Common Practices Existed at Their Institutions

"Rule" or Practice	*% Who Agreed*	*% Who Said It Affected Them*
There is a "pecking order" in which junior faculty are treated less respectfully than senior faculty.	59	32
Community service is less respected than research and publishing.	64	36
African American faculty who speak out about racism and cultural insensitivity in the Academy are labeled as "troublemakers."	50	43
Tenure can be denied to faculty who do not appear to "fit in" with their colleagues.	57	40
Tenure is often based on how well an African American faculty member is liked by his/her colleagues, regardless of the individual's scholarship, teaching record, and community service.	45	38

N = 136

ined additional descriptive statistics to learn more about the faculty who said African Americans who speak out about racism and cultural insensitivity are labeled as troublemakers we learned several interesting details. First, a slightly higher percentage of these respondents were dissatisfied at their institution and a much lower percentage than the percentage in the total sample were very satisfied at their current institution. Furthermore, whereas 38 percent of the respondents in the total sample did not plan to remain at their current institution, 55 percent of the faculty who worked at institutions at which African Americans were labeled as troublemakers planned to leave. Finally, a higher percentage of these faculty were the only Black faculty member in their department when compared to the total sample of respondents.

Two questionnaire items pertained to unwritten rules about tenure. The first statement said, "Tenure can be denied to faculty who do not appear to 'fit in' with their colleagues." Nearly 60 percent of the respondents indicated that this was an unwritten rule or common practice at their institution and 40 percent said that it had affected them on a personal level. As in the previous example, faculty who said that at their institution gaining tenure was tied to "fitting in" were less likely than the respondents in the total sample to be very satisfied at their institution. Additionally, as expected, a higher percentage tended to be junior faculty than the percentage in the total sample. Furthermore, whereas 17 percent of the respondents in the total sample had no Black department-level colleagues, 26 percent of these faculty did not.

The last statement said, "Tenure is often based on how well an African American faculty member is liked by his/her colleagues, regardless of the individual's scholarship, teaching record, and community service." Forty-five percent of the faculty agreed that this was a common practice at their institution and nearly 40 percent said it had affected them personally. When we examined additional descriptive statistics, we learned that faculty who worked at institutions where it was common for gaining tenure to be linked to being liked, instead of just on merit, were less likely to have been mentored than respondents in the total sample. Second, they were a lot less likely to be very satisfied at their current institution and more likely to be dissatisfied enough to leave. Whereas 17 percent of the respondents in the total sample were the only Blacks in their department, 27 percent of the faculty who worked at institutions at which being liked outweighed merit were the only Blacks in their department.

Summary

The process of demystifying the culture of the Academy and making expectations and unwritten rules clearer (Gregory, 1995) is an important piece of the puzzle that constitutes what is needed to increase Black faculty satisfaction, and thereby, retention rates (Alfred, 2001; Jarmon, 2001), particularly in PWIs. In our opinion, the process must start long before they are actually hired as faculty. We believe it should begin when they are students (Alfred, 2001; White & Siwatu, 2002). Unfortunately, barriers at every level of the education system, starting with the K-12 system, and the inequities that are embedded in U.S. society make this difficult.

Because America is a country of contrasts, in which we have the very rich and individuals and families who live in extreme poverty, African American and Latino families and children remain overrepresented among those living in poverty (U.S. Census Bureau, 2001). America also has a universal educational system that allows every American to attend public schools. However, the schools vary in quality (Oakes & Rogers, 2002). Students can gain an exemplary K-12 education or they can be "educated" in substandard schools that have a high percentage of underqualified teachers (Ingersoll, 1999). Poor students from all racial and ethnic groups are the most likely groups to attend substandard schools. Both poverty and a substandard K-12 education lead to an underrepresentation of these groups in higher education, especially graduate school—the pipeline that feeds the professorial ranks (Thompson, 1999). African Americans who are fortunate enough to make it to graduate school must contend with numerous factors that increase the likelihood that they will drop out (Thompson, 1999), including limited financial aid, and the paucity of research and teaching assistantships that are awarded to African American students. Woods (2001) said that mentoring could solve some of the problems that Black doctoral students experience, but many have difficulty finding willing mentors.

Regardless of why the disparity in the distribution of assistantships exists, the fact remains that it has undoubtedly served as an impediment to African American students at the graduate level. Moreover, it puts Black students at an even greater disadvantage than they already are. Nettles (1990) wrote, "Students with fellowships and assistantships are found to experience a greater amount of interaction with faculty, and the students who interact most with the faculty perform better and enjoy the greatest amount of satisfaction with their doctoral programs" (p. 516). Wilson (1988) stated, "The availability of fellowships also gives students access to research and publication opportunities. Where such opportunities are lacking, even with the possession of the Ph.D., blacks are less competitive for faculty positions" (p. 170).

Therefore, the issue of what can be done to improve the percentage of assistantships that are awarded to African American students is another area that should become a priority for postsecondary institutions, if they are truly committed to reversing the problem of African American underrepresentation at the doctoral level. Improving this situation might also ameliorate other problems. For example, if students who have assistantships are more likely than other students to interact with faculty, this would give African American students an opportunity to be mentored by faculty, and possibly learn some of the unwritten rules ahead of time that might eventually "make or break" their academic career. It might also change the perception that many faculty have of African American students and their culture, thereby broadening the knowledge base of non-Black faculty. More important, however, is the fact that assistantships might also increase the probability that these students will later find employment in higher education.

However, as the results that we presented in this chapter suggest, when many Black students successfully complete their graduate studies to enter the professoriate they find that the "plot thickens" (White & Siwatu, 2002). Few graduate programs have prepared them for the politics that are largely governed by the unwritten rules in the Academy. Like the Masons and other "secret societies," postsecondary institutions are full of mysteries that they must uncover (W. Watkins,

2002). These unwritten rules have served as invisible "gatekeepers" (W. Watkins, 2002) that can be detrimental to their efforts to gain tenure and job security.

Therefore, in order to increase Black faculty satisfaction in higher education, postsecondary institutions must identify the unwritten rules and make them explicit (Gregory, 1995), starting when students are in graduate school. Because, as we have noted in previous chapters, numerous Black faculty are unlikely to be assigned formal mentors who might teach them these unwritten rules, exposure to these rules should be embedded in the graduate school curriculum. This could occur through a regular course for all graduate students. The course could teach students about the politics, expectations, and unwritten rules governing many aspects of the Academy. This would decrease the likelihood of Black faculty and Black graduate students being ignorant about the "lay of the land" and feeling marginalized.

Again, mentoring—informal and formal—is an important determinant of the academic success of students and faculty of color. Ideally, mentoring should exist in and outside of the classroom. It should permit students to witness the totality of the profession, and the culture of higher education. This approach has been shown to (1) improve students' self-confidence to do professional work, (2) teach them how to cope with the formal and informal structures of the institution, and (3) foster respect and a desire to learn more about their mentor's selected field (M. Brown, Davis, & McClendon, 1999).

In the meantime, as long as the unwritten rules of the Academy remain shrouded in secrecy, current problems will persist. Some Black faculty will continue to feel marginalized (Jarmon, 2001) and even dissatisfied enough to leave. Full inclusion in higher education includes candor about the unwritten rules, in order to increase the likelihood that new faculty and junior faculty will be successful at their institution. This inclusion starts with the way in which Black graduate students are treated. Mentoring and providing Black graduate students with assistantships and opportunities to work closely with faculty (Alfred, 2001; Jarmon, 2001), and then providing newly hired Black faculty with all of the pieces of the puzzle that constitute a supportive work environment, are necessary so that the Academy, particularly PWIs, will seem less like a "foreign land" to them and more like a place where they can thrive.

As we mentioned in a previous chapter, Dr. Freeman Hrabowski, president of the University of Maryland, Baltimore County, has developed an approach to diversity that illustrates what can happen when the Academy makes a concerted effort to become more inclusive. Through the Meyerhoff Scholars Program, which targets high-achieving high school students, the university has created a formula for academic success that increases the likelihood that these students will be well prepared to earn graduate degrees in math, science, and engineering, and possibly join the ranks of the professoriate. In addition to high expectations and a rigorous curriculum, mentoring and working closely with undergraduate faculty are integral components of the program (Hrabowski, 1999, 2001). Thus the program and its underlying philosophy that students of color have the potential to do outstanding work and can succeed in fields where people of color are grossly underrepresented—not only as students but also among the professoriate—are models from which the Academy can learn much.

5

COPING WITH CULTURAL INSENSITIVITY AND SOMETIMES JUST PLAIN STUPIDITY IN THE ACADEMY

IN THE MURKY WATERS that constitute race relations in the United States, there is often a thin line between what is deemed acceptable and what is viewed as unacceptable. Sometimes, behaviors or comments that end up being offensive originate from innocence and ignorance (Thompson, 2004b). For example, many years ago, during her undergraduate years, one of us spent a summer working as an intern news reporter in a city where African Americans were scarce. During this time, she experienced many upsetting incidents. A few of these incidents unequivocably qualified as blatant racism; others constituted cultural insensitivity—less offensive incidents that were perpetrated by individuals who may have meant no harm and may have acted out of ignorance, yet the incidents can still be harmful.

A good example took place in the newsroom one day when a colleague, a lively and friendly White woman, asked the author, and her biracial roommate (who was half Black and half White) if she could "feel their hair." She then placed one hand on each young woman's head and exclaimed, "Ooh! It feels just like Brillo!" Because the author and her roommate were both young college undergraduates who were in town to complete summer journalism internships, they were unsure of how to respond. They were quite offended, but did not tell their colleague that they were, perhaps primarily because they believed she meant no harm. They also believed that she was unaware that they viewed her behavior as culturally insensitive at the very least. Moreover, as a senior reporter and full-time member of the newspaper staff, the woman was in a position of authority over them, which meant she could have jeopardized their jobs at the newspaper. So, there was probably an element of fear behind their silence.

This incident paled in comparison to a blatantly racist act that the same author and her roommate experienced while walking to work one day that summer. They were in a crosswalk when the driver, a White man, of a car that had inched menacingly close to the young women, yelled out the window "[N word], next time, I'm gonna run you over!" The combination of his words, tone, and the evil look on his face left no doubt in their minds; this man was racist and could seriously harm them.

In *Through Ebony Eyes: What Teachers Need to Know but Are Afraid to Ask about African American Students*, Thompson (2004b) wrote, "when it comes to race relations and cultural sensitivity, there are clearly defined taboos. . . . However, there are also gray areas—lesser known topics, words, and actions that may or may not be considered racist, culturally insensitive, or culturally offensive. It is often the gray areas that cause a problem" (p. 212).

Although cultural insensitivity may stem from ignorance and innocence, and may be less overt, and appear to be less offensive and seemingly less harmful than racist acts, its effects cannot be underestimated. A good example involved the Getty Museum in Los Angeles. In July 2004, a culturally sensitive situation arose as a result of the actions of a volunteer tour guide for a group of elementary students who were on a field trip. As she was explaining the differences between "smooth and rough textures in stonework and other materials," the guide "rubbed two black students' heads and . . . described their hair as rough. Parents and teachers said the students . . . thought they were being ridiculed and that the docent was invoking racial stereotypes" (Daniels, 2004, p. B4). A fourth-grade teacher who witnessed the incident stated, "The kids were in shock. It was like she had just ripped out their spirits" (p. B4). After meeting with several community-based groups, including school district representatives, museum officials apologized for the guide's behavior. However, some community representatives believed that they did not go far enough, because the guide was still permitted to conduct tours after the apology was issued (Daniels, 2004).

Unfortunately, cultural insensitivity and racism are no strangers to the Academy. As African American faculty, we (the authors) have experienced both racism, a topic that we will discuss in depth in the next chapter, and cultural insensitivity. In fact, one of us had an early encounter with a woman who would become her department chair that foreshadowed the rampant cultural insensitivity and racism that she would later experience at a PWI where she eventually became dissatisfied enough to leave. It started during her job interview.

As a part of the interview for her very first faculty position in higher education, the author had a meeting with her future chair, a White woman. After giving a presentation to the seven faculty members in the department and feeling like she had done a good job of answering questions, she was ushered into the chair's office. After the niceties of asking about each other's health, the chair went into her "department chair mode," using a high-pitched and disparaging tone. As she sat behind her desk, she held a pencil in her hand, ready to take notes when the interviewee responded. She said nothing about the program for which the woman was interviewing, the schedule, or about the presentation she had just seen. Instead, she told the candidate about her own accomplishments and spoke about her expectations, should the author be hired. Then, the department chair gave the candidate an example of the type of class she might be teaching and the teaching load, but her description and tone were very condescending. When she described the classes, how often they met, and the times, she remarked, "If we decide to hire you here, you'll have to show up for classes on time. You cannot be late under any circumstances. Also, you must show up! If your class is on a Tuesday, you have to be here on Tuesday."

Obviously, her idea of the interview was to tell the author that tardiness would not be tolerated. The question is why did the chair assume that attendance and punctuality would be problematic for her? They had just met, and the candidate had been on time for her presentation and interview. Had the chair already internalized the stereotype that Blacks are always late, or had she previously had problems with lateness and absenteeism from other faculty? Because the author believed that the department chair's words and condescending tone stemmed from cultural ignorance and insensitivity, this was the beginning of a difficult relationship. From that point on, the author and chair would have numerous encounters that left the author feeling that the chair was culturally insensitive, at the very least. The most blatant was when the chair refused to intervene after a Ku Klux Klan member, a student in the author's class, threatened the author, who eventually had to get a restraining order against him.

Because both of us, the authors, have experienced cultural insensitivity and racism at various PWIs where we have worked, we wanted to give the participants in our study an opportunity to describe their own experiences. Therefore, in this chapter, we present the questionnaire results pertaining to cultural insensitivity. For the purposes of this study, cultural insensitivity refers to less offensive incidents and comments that display ignorance or negativity about Blacks and black culture but that do not qualify as racism. However, the consequences can still be harmful.

Results

Although 16 percent of the questionnaire respondents agreed that cultural insensitivity was uncommon at their institution, 84 percent disagreed. Additional questionnaire items pertaining to cultural insensitivity were designed to determine whether or not participants had experienced cultural insensitivity from their colleagues, immediate supervisor, non-chair and non-dean administrators, and students.

Cultural Insensitivity from Students

Eighteen percent of the faculty who completed the survey said they had never experienced cultural insensitivity from any of their students. However, 82 percent said they had. The two predictors that surfaced through regression analysis revealed that faculty who said they had never experienced cultural insensitivity from students were more likely than others to say (1) the racial climate at their institution had not caused stress for them, and (2) they had never experienced cultural insensitivity from any administrator.

Comments from the faculty whom we interviewed for the current study suggest that cultural insensitivity from students could surface either directly or indirectly. Direct manifestations occurred when students were overtly rude or disrespectful to Black faculty, and this rudeness and disrespect appeared to be racially motivated. However, sometimes, the cultural insensitivity was barely perceptible, because of its indirectness. For example, several interviewees mentioned that some students took the liberty of addressing them in a less formal manner than they addressed non-Black faculty. In other cases, the cultural insensitivity was more blatant. For example, one interviewee, a Black professor at an institution in Georgia, described an incident between himself and a White female student that could have escalated into a situation that cost him his job. He explained how actions and discussions that may appear to be innocent when White professors are involved can be perceived very differently when the professor in question is a Black male, and thus create a culturally tense situation that may even border on racism. According to this interviewee:

> Recently, I had an incident where I feel like a White female student basically pathologized me and tried to play the race card, and the whole male–female dynamic and the White-female–Black-male issue of me trying to harm her in some way when this young lady

and I had only had words in public. . . . We'd only spoken. It never got physical; it was just some verbiage that passed back and forth between the two of us, and what she did was she behaved in a way that was threatening to me. She started crying and running down the hall, you know, the whole routine. She created a big scene and I was her supervisor, [which] made it seem as though I was threatening to her and in return, I took it as her threatening me—that she was threatening my personal reputation and professional reputation. It's the whole ball of wax of a Black man pursuing this White female type of thing, so I resigned from the situation. I refused to work with her because it was almost like screaming "rape."

The indirect manifestation can occur when there are interracial conflicts between Black and non-Black students or between Black students and non-Black faculty, and Black faculty are expected to intervene. For example, according to a female interviewee:

The African American students who have problems with several professors would be students that they ended up giving to me. When the student was given to me as an independent graduate studies student, I took over and stood up for the student. The faculty member who moved over and allowed the department to give me this student felt that I could deal with her better, as other faculty members were not willing to give her a chance.

This same professor described another example, illustrating that Black faculty are sometimes expected to intervene when culturally sensitive situations arise between Black students and professors. She said:

One situation was when an African American student had words with an [Asian] professor. The professor didn't know how to respond, so she went to another professor who was a senior Latino faculty member. They suggested the [Asian] professor go to an African American faculty member for no other reason but simply because she was African American. The [Asian] professor wanted the African American faculty member to resolve the issue.

Cultural Insensitivity from Colleagues

Seventeen percent of the faculty who completed the questionnaire said they had never experienced any cultural insensitivity from their colleagues; 83 percent said they had. A stepwise multiple regression equation produced four predictors of how faculty responded to the statement about cultural insensitivity from colleagues. The strongest predictor pertained to their relations with their immediate supervisor. Faculty who had never been subjected to cultural insensitivity from their department chair or dean were very likely to say they had never experienced it from colleagues either. The second strongest predictor pertained to racism. Faculty who had never experienced racism from their colleagues were also likely to state they had not experienced any cultural insensitivity from them either. The third predictor indicated that faculty who worked at institutions at which cultural insensitivity was uncommon were unlikely to have experienced it from colleagues. Finally, faculty who had never experienced cultural insensitivity from non–department chair and non-dean administrators also were unlikely to have been subjected to it from their colleagues.

Comments from interviewees gave us additional feedback. For example, a professor from California described a colleague whose tone and attitude exuded cultural insensitivity and at times, even racism. She said:

> I have experienced cultural insensitivity from one particular colleague at my current institution, which is in a metropolitan area of southern California. Our service community is a very large urban school district. So it's in that context I would like to describe the insensitivity. I've experienced it and I've observed it in dealing with others. I was hired with another woman of color and our fellow colleague is a White person. Repeatedly, we have experienced insensitivity because of how she talked to our students and treated us. We felt patronized. Quite often, we have felt talked down to, as though she expected us not to understand and that she would need to explain a lot of things. We also found that she was resistant to being

supervised by us or having either of us coordinate the program, even when I served in a position of authority. I [was responsible] for a national program review, and joint state review. She was totally resistant to cooperating with me, to any suggestions, or to innovations I might make. I found after the situation became untenable and administration was contacted, they were reluctant to believe that a person could be racist. They wanted to attribute all of the problems—the lack of her cooperation—to anything except racism, even though we had discovered a pattern. She cooperated with White colleagues throughout the college on various committees. Others were not experiencing what I and the other colleague of color had experienced. So, I found that the dean and associate dean were very reluctant to acknowledge our concerns and allegations that there must have been racism. One department chair seemed willing to accept that there must be some cultural insensitivity at work. The worst was when I was serving as the chair for the National State Review and the person refused to come to the meetings and do her part of the work. The administration felt that they could not compel her, although all the other participants in the programs were required to participate and cooperate.

A professor, who taught at a southern university, said that differences between Black and White styles of discourse can create culturally charged situations between Black and White faculty. He explained:

I'd like to discuss a general theme that I've realized as a minority faculty working in a predominantly White institution. The largest theme I seemed to have recognized and that seems to be a problem and an issue for me as well as other Black faculty members is the issue of communication. I think that the core of who we are as people and at the core of our differences racially, there are specific communication differences. I think that in the African American community, we communicate on one level or in one manner and that is true of White faculty. They communicate in a different way.

I think that those communication differences—those core fundamental communication differences—create issues and misunderstandings and are instances of insensitivity. I think that the dominant culture—White dominant culture—is insensitive to our communication style, and that what they want is for us to be more like them. When we don't personify their method of communication, their methods of style (and it's not just verbal communication; it's physical communication and every other aspect of the communication genre), I don't know whether they're threatened by it or, whether or not it's just that they don't understand. So, it's labeled as something that's not of value. Typically, it's labeled as "unprofessional." The way you respond as a minority faculty member is often considered unprofessional and the context of professionalism is totally based on what they prescribed as professionalism. That's the number one thing I've seen from a broad perspective and I can take that particular issue and nail it down to some specifics where I've had instances where I've commented or not commented. Sometimes it's not even what you say; sometimes it's what you don't say, where I've either made comments or not commented, and my comment or lack of a comment was perceived as being unprofessional.

Another professor, who had worked at a PWI for several years, provided a detailed explanation of one of numerous examples of cultural insensitivity that he had experienced at his university. According to this professor:

I was on the Doctoral Program Committee at our university and the issue of trying to recruit and retain more African Americans and other students of color into the doctoral program came up. So, I gave an example of what I thought needed to be changed, which [was] basically about attitudes about people and relationships. I gave this example: This is a true story that happened about three years ago. Through my contacts in the community, an African American gentleman sought me out. He made an appointment and came to see me and told me that he was shopping for a doctoral program. He was interested in our program. We talked about the program at our university. In the process of doing this, we struck up a nice conversation. We had been talking about 40 minutes when there was a tap on my door. It was a colleague, who when I opened the door, peered in, saw him and saw me, and said, "Excuse me. We're next door having a conference. Could you and your friend keep down your voices and your laughter?" I said, "Okay, I think I can do that," and closed the door. We looked at each other and the gentleman never applied and never came back.

So, I told this story to the committee. They looked at me and said, "What was the problem with that?" "Well," I said, "let's just look at a couple of levels of it. First of all, this was not someone who was a friend of mine. Secondly, there is obviously a need to respect people's spaces, but the assumption coming in was that some friend of mine had dropped by and we were having a personal conversation. Thirdly, the person who did it never inquired about what was going on with us or, quite frankly cared." I told them that it has been my experience that when people of color seek out other faculty of color, and there aren't very many of those, when they feel they can establish a relationship, it makes the difference between coming and not coming [to that particular university].

Another interviewee said that his colleagues' preoccupation with his clothing was an ongoing culturally insensitive situation that he faced. His comments suggest that what may be perceived as innocent and even complimentary statements by non-Blacks, may have the opposite effect on Blacks. He stated:

For me personally, there are comments made constantly about something or another. You know, I'm constantly getting some type of little comment here or there. The one thing that stands out the most is something having to do with my clothing, that I'm always so well dressed. It's like the total emphasis in my life is on my clothing, which is hardly the case. But there seems to be a lot of focus from my colleagues on my apparel. They seem to take notice of my clothing and refer to me as the "best dressed person in the department." What they don't understand is that I can't show up in jeans and a T-shirt. I can't come in jeans and a sweatshirt because the moment I do that, I'm reduced to being nothing more than at best a student. At best! White faculty can show up in jeans and a T-shirt or sweatshirt and they can still be Dr. whoever it is that they are. The students still see them that way. They're still respected that way. The moment I show up in anything other than a shirt and tie or professional dress, I'm deemed or viewed as at best, a student. Now, "at best" means that I could be a maintenance person, or I might be, you know, the copy guy. That's why I said, "At best a student." So "at best" gets me there, but I'm definitely not Dr. _____. I'm definitely not considered as Dr. _____. Does that make sense? That is the best example I can give. In response, I'd normally just say "Thank you; I appreciate that" or when I get the comments I've recently just started saying, "I can't wear the same thing that you wear, because I wouldn't get the same treatment you get if I wore that."

Another interviewee noted that her colleagues' insensitivity was not necessarily related to her race or culture, but to the fact that she was a native of Louisiana. She said, "I don't want to generalize, but there are certain individuals who feel that it's okay to refer to me in inappropriate terms which refer to my culture. For instance, my parents are from Louisiana. So [as] a nickname, a certain colleague feels it's okay to refer to me as 'Voodoo.' I specifically spoke to the individual and told him not to refer to me as that because it is totally unacceptable."

Another interviewee said that her colleagues' cultural insensitivity surfaced through comments about her professionalism. According to this professor

Colleagues second-guess what I've said. Because I'm at an auxiliary site, I would have conflicts with colleagues but it would be by phone. When someone would doubt something that I've said, they would make comments like, 'Don't take this personally,' and I'd call them on that. They always expect me to have to show specific references, which to me meant they were questioning my professionalism.

Several interviewees described examples of cultural insensitivity that stemmed from colleagues making negative comments about Black students or about diversity-related courses. For example, a professor who taught in Oregon said, "There have been instances in Portland where they've made statements. I teach the Multicultural Urban Education course, and many of my colleagues are extremely happy that they don't have to teach this course. They feel that it is difficult because its mostly dealing with racism, sexism, and gender biases." A male professor said, "It has not been overt, basically just making general comments about African American students who are undesirable or unsuccessful. When they speak, they focus on this group of students as though they're [unaware] of those who are successful."

Cultural Insensitivity from Administrators

Thirty-eight percent of the questionnaire respondents said they had never experienced any cultural insensitivity from their department chair or dean, but 62 percent said they had. Through multiple regression analysis, we identified six predictors of faculty responses to the statement about cultural insensitivity from a chair or dean. Four of the predictors pertained to other aspects of cultural insensitivity and racism, and two were related to feeling valued. The strongest predictor showed that faculty who had never experienced racism from their chair or dean were unlikely to have experienced cultural insensitivity from their immediate supervisor either. Second, faculty who had never been subjected to cultural insensitivity from their colleagues were unlikely to have experienced it from their immediate supervisor. The third predictor revealed that faculty who worked at institutions where their experiences were valued and respected by their colleagues, chair, and dean also tended to have culturally sensitive immediate supervisors. Fourth, faculty who had not experienced cultural insensitivity from non-chair and non-dean administrators were unlikely to have culturally insensitive immediate supervisors. Furthermore, faculty who had never experienced any racism from their students had a higher probability of having a culturally sensitive department chair or dean.

Finally, faculty who worked at institutions where their contributions were valued and respected by their colleagues, chair, and dean tended to also have culturally sensitive immediate supervisors.

Whereas 38 percent of the questionnaire respondents said they had never experienced any cultural insensitivity from an immediate supervisor, 30 percent said they had never been subjected to it from other non-chair or non-dean administrators. Seventy percent disagreed.

Through regression analysis, we identified several predictors of how faculty responded to this questionnaire item. Each factor pertained to racism or cultural insensitivity. The strongest predictor indicated that the faculty who were least likely to have experienced cultural insensitivity from non-chair and non-dean administrators were the ones who had never experienced any racism from other administrators at their current institution. Additionally, faculty who had never experienced cultural insensitivity from their colleagues, students, or immediate supervisor were unlikely to have experienced it from other university administrators. Finally, faculty who stated they had never experienced any racism from their students were unlikely to have experienced cultural insensitivity from any (non-chair or non-dean) administrator. Table 5.1 contains a summary of the questionnaire results pertaining to cultural insensitivity.

Summary

Throughout this book so far, cultural insensitivity and racism have surfaced as factors that were related to Black faculty satisfaction or dissatisfaction at their current institution. These problems were related to whether or not faculty felt respected, whether or not they believed they worked in a supportive environment, and their beliefs and experiences pertaining to the unwritten rules of the Academy. In this chapter, we looked more closely at the participants' experiences with cultural insensitivity. We learned that the majority worked at institutions at which cultural insensitivity was common from students, faculty, and administrators. A recurring theme was that faculty who felt

TABLE 5.1
Faculty's Experiences with Cultural Insensitivity by Percentage

Statement	Agree	Disagree
At my current institution, I have never experienced any cultural insensitivity from my faculty colleagues.	17	83
At my current institution, I have never experienced any cultural insensitivity from my immediate supervisor, such as my department chair or dean.	38	62
At my current institution, I have never experienced any cultural insensitivity from any non-chair or non-dean administrator.	30	70
At my current institution, I have never experienced any cultural insensitivity from any of my students.	18	82
Cultural insensitivity is uncommon at my institution.	16	84

$N = 136$

supported and valued were unlikely to say they had experienced cultural insensitivity. Moreover, faculty who had experienced cultural insensitivity or racism from one segment of the university community were more likely to have experienced it from others. This suggests that when cultural insensitivity is not combated at one level, it can flourish and become pervasive throughout the entire campus community.

Another theme that emerged in this chapter is one that has been evident in previous ones: "Leadership makes the difference" (T. Brown, 1995; Lipman-Blumen, 2005; 1998; Thompson, 2003). The faculty's experiences with and perceptions of university leaders, especially their immediate supervisor, were related to their overall level of satisfaction at their current institution. This theme and the need for institutions to become more culturally sensitive will surface again in the remaining chapters of this book, especially in the next one, when we present the results of our study pertaining specifically to racism.

In *Cultural Proficiency: A Manual for School Leaders,* Lindsey, Nuri Robins, and Terrell (1999) defined "cultural proficiency" and explained how educational leaders can become culturally proficient and improve organizational climates. The authors presented a six-point continuum that requires leaders to examine behaviors, beliefs, actions, and policies within institutions. The continuum starts with "cultural destructiveness," which consists of practices and policies that are detrimental to individuals from marginalized groups. The second level, "cultural incapacity," occurs when individuals' interactions with marginalized groups result in subordination to the dominant culture. The third point on the continuum, "cultural blindness" is exhibited by individuals who believe that race and culture make no difference and all people are the same. Fourth, "cultural pre-competence" occurs when individuals become aware of the limitations that often occur when people from different cultures try to communicate and interact with each other. Fifth, "cultural competence" takes place when individuals accept and respect cultural differences, continually assess their own cultural knowledge and beliefs, and make various adaptations of their own belief systems, policies, and practices. Finally, "cultural proficiency" occurs when individuals within organizations master the essential elements of cultural competence and are able to use them appropriately in a variety of cultural settings. According to Lindsey et al. (1999), one of the essential elements of a culturally proficient faculty is valuing diversity. However, the presumption of entitlement, and ignorance about the need to change policies and behaviors that are culturally destructive, become barriers to cultural proficiency.

The results that we presented in this chapter suggest the Academy has a long way to go in order for cultural proficiency to become the norm in higher education among students, faculty, and administrators. In the next chapter, we will go a step further by looking deeply at racism, which can become the evil offspring of cultural insensitivity.

6

THE "R WORD"

Facing Racism's Ugly Reality in the Academy

THE HISTORY OF RACISM in higher education is as old as the U.S. Academy itself. The Academy's racist legacy includes such facts as that African Americans and Jews were once prohibited from attending most PWIs (Fleming, 1976). Later, many northern universities instituted a quota system that permitted a limited number of students who had previously been barred from attending PWIs to enroll (Davie, 1949; Duberman, 1989; Ravitch, 1983). In the South, this was not the case. Many PWIs preferred to send Black students North for an education, instead of permitting them to enroll (Davie, 1949). However, even when northern universities accepted Black students for admission, these students often faced blatant racism. For example, in the late 1800s, W. E. B. DuBois received his bachelor's from Harvard cum laude, followed by his master's one year later, and the PhD in 1895 (S. Watkins, 1944). According to Lewis (1993), in his earlier writings, DuBois spoke favorably about faculty members such as George Santayana and William James, as well as his experiences at Harvard, but in his later writings he spoke negatively about Harvard. Despite the fact that DuBois won two oratorical contests, scholarships, and the honor of being named one of the commencement day speakers, racism made it difficult for him to feel at ease at Harvard, even after a professor reprimanded a White student for refusing to sit next to him in class. According to Lewis (1993), "DuBois was never capable of mixing comfortably with his white classmates. The few efforts he made left bruises" (p. 97).

Today, although it may be less common than in previous eras, blatant racism surfaces periodically in the Academy, and covert racism permeates the institutional climate of many institutions (Gregory, 1995; Turner & Myers, 2000; West, 2002; White & Siwatu, 2002). For example, several years ago, when an African American graduate student (a friend of one of the authors of this book) asked her professor if class would be cancelled in honor of the Martin Luther King Jr. holiday, to show his displeasure, the White professor disparagingly referred to the student—one of the few African Americans in the class—as "Little Miss Buckwheat," in reference to the African American boy on the "Little Rascals" film series whose hair was often uncombed.

More recently, as we noted previously, one of us was seriously contemplating leaving her PWI after, among other things, a young White student employee threatened to call security on her when she refused to move her students to another classroom. Several months later, a racially charged controversy erupted in the college community at which this same author worked. It started with the burning of an art project—a cross—by a small group of students who later claimed they did not know the historical significance of cross burning. Next, the N word was scrawled on a poster depicting George Washington Carver. Thereafter, racial tensions began to escalate and a sense of unease spread throughout the community that houses the consortia of colleges where this author works. The climax came when a White professor claimed her car had been vandalized and spray painted with racist, sexist, and anti-Semitic graffiti. After classes were cancelled and a huge multiethnic rally was held in support of the professor, law enforcement officials said the professor had perpetrated a hoax; she had vandalized her own car—a crime for which she was later convicted.

Upon learning this, the campus community appeared to breathe a collective sigh of relief. During a conversation that one of us had with a former dean at the college where the professor who vandalized her own car worked, the former dean told the author, "I knew it was a hoax all along. Our students are good. They could never do anything that's racist." As the former dean continued to speak, he made it clear to the author that he believed that racism was a thing of the past. This man is not alone. Many Whites, including administrators, professors, and students, and even conservative Blacks are in denial about the existence of racism and delude themselves into believing that we live in a "colorblind" society (Thompson, 2004b). Regarding racism in the larger society and workforce, Tony Brown (1995) said, "Whites may not feel comfortable being upfront about racial differences, but they can see the inefficiency in the time and energy spent pretending to ignore such differences" (pp. 219–220). Hrabowski et al. (1998) wrote, "race . . . is a hot topic—one of those topics we have difficulty discussing and which quickly leads to tension and feelings of discomfort" (p. vii). However, Toth (2002b) spoke specifically about racism in the Academy when she wrote:

> few White people, however well-intentioned, know how deeply racism pervades the lives of African Americans—from random name calling, to assumptions of prowess in music and sports and nothing else, to routine police harassment just for being in certain areas ("driving while black"). By the time [a Black professor] is hired at a university, she will have endured constant insinuations that she got where she is through affirmative action, not through her own merits. She will also have been told that racism is no longer a factor in academia. ([I] call this "epistemological solipsism": If I don't know about it, it doesn't exist). (pp. 1–2)

White said that both students and faculty can experience racism, but it is often subtle. "Nobody is going to burn a cross on your lawn," he warned. "Nobody is going to openly call you names. They do little stuff" (White & Siwatu, 2002, p. 88).

In his autobiography, Salome Thomas-El (2003) described numerous blatantly racist incidents that he experienced as an undergraduate student at East Stroudsburg University in Pennsylvania. While living in the dormitory during freshman year, in addition to treating them like pariahs, White students made many attempts to drive Thomas-El and another African American student out of the university, including placing a sign that said "Go home [N word]" and painting a swastika on Thomas-El's door. The harassment occurred so frequently that Thomas-El often wanted to drop out of college, but each time he reached this level of despair, his mother convinced him to stay.

Unfortunately, the harassment was not limited to racist students. Like the students, one professor, in particular, engaged in racist behavior. Because he believed that Blacks are inherently inferior to Whites, the professor gave Black students low grades that they did not earn, made negative remarks about them, criticized the way they spoke, and even tried to convince them that they did not belong at the university. Eventually, Thomas-El came to a painful realization: "No matter what I did in that man's classroom, my work would never be acceptable to him" (p. 64).

After learning that this professor had a history of treating Black students unfairly, Thomas-El confronted him. He warned the professor that he would no longer tolerate his abuse. Thereafter, the professor stopped the harassment. However, one of the saddest aspects of this story is that the professor's racist behavior appeared to be well known among his colleagues and to administrators. Nevertheless, they were slow in acting on the victimized students' behalf. This behavior is a common characteristic of weak leaders in the Academy, who turn a blind eye to racism and cultural insensitivity, and thereby allow these problems to become embedded in the institutional culture.

In addition to underscoring the fact that racism is prevalent in the Academy, we need to make two additional points about racism. First, there are two types of racists: liberals and conservatives. According to author and nationally known television talk show host Tony Brown, "Conservative racists block the door to opportunity. Liberal racists stifle Black self-reliance" (T. Brown, 1995, p. 125). Both types are destructive to African Americans. As Brown stated, "Centuries of racist treatment have helped impose a permanent second-class status on much of the Black community" (p. 224). "Once a group is marginalized, it is easily scapegoated. Blacks have been reminded of this frequently in recent times" (pp. 128–129).

Second, Blacks are not the only group that can be victims of racism. In "Racism on the Tenure Track," Jayate (2002) described his experiences with racism as a newly hired tenure-track professor in the South. Jayate, who specialized in South Asian philosophical and religious traditions, said that he was subjected to racism by his department chair and from at least one colleague. He wrote, "within a month [of accepting the job], it became painfully apparent that we [Jayate and his family] were strangers in a strange land. . . . Very quickly the battle lines were drawn: I was the interloper whose skills, expectations, and color [were] sending ripples into the placid (and poisoned) lake of [the university]" (p. 1). The situation worsened when Jayate's department chair started to openly treat him disrespectfully. "In order to assert his superiority," Jayate wrote, "my chairman began calling me 'boy' in public, in front of students, and in private" (p. 1). Then, a tenured colleague started to treat Jayate disrespectfully in front of students and even threatened to use violence against him. By spring, Jayate realized that his chair and colleagues had not only started to ignore him, but they also excluded him from discussions and course planning. Soon, they had taken away all of his advisees. When the chair told him that he would be fired, Jayate became proactive. After realizing that he had grounds for a racial discrimination lawsuit and that he planned to pursue it, university officials compromised. Instead of firing Jayate, they permitted him to resign and gave him an additional year's salary.

Jayate's experiences at this university underscore the fact that racism is alive and well in the Academy. However, when it is exposed, often the victim is perceived as problematic, instead of the Academy facing itself—warts and all. Because we (the authors) have both seen evidence of racism in higher education, we wanted to learn more about the experiences of other Black faculty. This topic is important, because as Rankin (2002) maintained, a racist campus environment is harmful to the entire institution. "When the campus environment is racially hostile or specifically anti-African American," he argued, "learning for all students becomes impaired and the overall educational process may stall or cease" (p. 75). Therefore, in this chapter, we present the results of our study describing the participants' experiences with racism at their current institution. Four questionnaire items were designed to measure whether or not participants had experienced racism at their current institution from their faculty colleagues, immediate supervisors, non-chair and non-dean administrators, and students. Other questionnaire items gave participants opportunities to talk about whether or not racism was common or uncommon at their institution, how they and administrators handled racist incidents, whether or not racism affected their job satisfaction, and whether or not the racial climate at work had caused stress for them. Finally, we gave participants an opportunity to discuss whether or not they had ever received unfair teaching evaluations, a problem that may or may not stem from racism, and one that other groups may experience.

Results

The Prevalence of Racism

As we noted in the previous chapter, only 16 percent of the questionnaire respondents said that cultural insensitivity was uncommon at their current institution. When asked about racism, 15 percent of the study participants stated that it was uncommon, but 84 percent said that it was common at their institution. Through stepwise multiple regression analysis, we identified several predictors of how faculty responded. We learned that faculty who worked at institutions at which cultural insensitivity was uncommon were more likely than others to also say that racism was uncommon at their institution. The second strongest predictor pertained to students. Faculty who had never experienced racism from students tended to state that racism was uncommon at their current institution. Third, faculty who agreed that the racial climate at their institution had not caused stress for them were likely to work at institutions where racism was uncommon. Furthermore, faculty who worked at institutions where racism was uncommon were unlikely to have experienced any cultural insensitivity from their department chair or dean. Finally, faculty at institutions where racism was uncommon were more likely than others to say they had never felt that any administrator was trying to undermine them at their current institution.

The feedback from faculty whom we interviewed for this study provides more details about why they believed that racism was common or uncommon at their current institution. For example, a professor who taught in the Southeast gave several examples to illustrate why she believed racism was common:

> In an area [of the university] called "Little Dixie," they say insensitive stuff all the time. They'll make the comment that "This is not directed at you" or something like that. Once, a teacher made a comment in a class to this Black student. The Black student who was [questioning] the instructor responded. The instructor's response was, "How would you feel if I said you were acting like Sambo?" At this site, we have very few Blacks; [there are] about 260 now, which is a large number for us. When something real blatant like that is said [tensions] go up, and others share things that they have heard. These things are common because it's in the Southeast. There has never been a Black person to live on [our] campus.

Another faculty member said that racist behavior was common among some constituents of her institution but uncommon among others. She explained:

> In terms of the student body and . . . whether racism emerges among and between the student body, that certainly is not uncommon. That's actually quite common. In terms of insensitivity from administration, I actually think that they do a great job of trying to be

sensitive and trying to promote diversity and trying to increase numbers, etc. Of course, things come out and things emerge, and there are issues that I think . . . have racial undertones. I think the administration does a good job though of trying to at least be aware of that and address that. But in terms of the student body, it is not uncommon at all. There was just recently a very bad racial incident where one student called another one [the N word] and the Black kid was cut up very badly and facing a large crowd of White students. He got beaten up. He got cut up very badly. That's kind of one of the most blatant things that just recently happened. But then there are other things all the time. Students say all the time "Black students shouldn't be here. They're not smart enough. They're just here, want a free ride," you know, that sort of thing. So that's very common.

A male professor maintained that racism is pervasive at all PWIs. According to this interviewee:

I think racism is inherent [in] all institutions, particularly predominantly White institutions. I think it's inherent; it's there. Basically, I have a lot of conversations with other minority faculty at my university and it's an issue of kind of like sleeping with the enemy, kind of like being in a relationship with someone who you know is abusive and you know at any moment in time they might turn on you. You know it's a guarantee. The only issue is when? But you know it's gonna happen. You know it's gonna happen. The only people I think it doesn't happen to, the only minorities that I think it doesn't happen to, are the people who are completely acquiescent to the system and who they don't view as a threat in any way, form, or fashion, the Uncle Toms. But the moment that you have a voice or the moment that you are recognized for anything on any level of success, then the likelihood that you are going to be victimized, torn down, or discriminated against, rises.

A professor who was somewhat unsure about whether or not racism was uncommon at her current institution, but who gave several examples indicating that it was common, stated:

I don't know if it's uncommon at this institution. . . . The policy of our institution on admission . . . would have disfavored the admissions of undergraduate students of color, particularly Latinos and Blacks. I found it amazingly insensitive [because it's in a] community that serves a very large urban community where Latinos and Blacks heavily populate adjacent communities. . . . So, I was very surprised to discover that it reached all the way to the administration, even though they articulate policies of diversity. . . . From my students, I've seen it, but not directly towards me, particularly, [through] some of the comments and resistance and some of the activities where we would deal with issues of race and cultural sensitivity and proficiency. I find it . . . belittling to . . . Black students when some of the literature . . . generalizes that all racial groups that have come to America have had problems trying to adjust. So, I find some of that resistance . . . when I hear comments from some of the students. I can't remember when it's [been] directed at me, but I have seen students select one professor over me, where I would have been the [most qualified] person . . . by reason of expertise. So. I think sometimes, those are subtle ways they show their racism as they will prefer the only White professor, even though my area of expertise would cover the subject matter for the master's degree.

In explaining how one single incident can convey strong messages about an institution's racial climate, another interviewee said:

This year, when I was going up North on vacation, I found a noose in a tree in the public square. I saw it early in the summer and I reported it to student services. About a month later, when I returned, it was still there. I then reported it to the dean who further reported it to student services or said he reported it. However it was at least eight weeks later that I walked through the square and it was still there. I felt that this prolonged time that it took to remove the noose sent a pretty clear message.

Racism from Students

Whereas 18 percent of the faculty said they had never experienced any cultural insensitivity from their students, 23 percent said they had never experienced any racism from them. However, 74 percent said they had. A multiple regression equation produced several predictors of responses to the statement about experiencing racism from students. As to be expected, the strongest predictor pertained to cultural insensitivity from students. Faculty who said they had never experienced cultural insensitivity from their students were the most likely participants to state that they had not experienced racism from students. The second strongest predictor revealed that faculty who had not experienced racism from their department chair or dean were unlikely to have experienced it from students. Third, faculty who stated that the racial climate at their institution had not affected their job satisfaction were unlikely to say that students had acted in racist ways toward them. The last predictor underscored the importance of feeling valued and respected. Faculty who said their experiences were valued and respected by their colleagues, chair, and dean were unlikely to have experienced racism from students.

Comments from several interviewees described behaviors or incidents that they perceived to be racist. For example, a professor, who worked in North Carolina, said that although he had not experienced racism from faculty or staff, an incident with a White student illustrated one of the challenges that he faced as a Black man at his university. He explained:

> We have this one student who certainly fits that image that you see on television—the bald, big guy with the redneck kind of image. . . . This is one of those guys who had issues dealing with women and anybody who wasn't Anglo Saxon White. I've had students tell me a lot of [things] about this guy and ironically this guy used to work for the university and tried to get a job on our campus police department. But one particular night, I was on campus fairly late and left, and realized when I got home that I'd left some work that I needed to review. So I [went] back to campus and had changed clothes and was looking pretty much like a student [wearing] a cap and some sweats. It was kind of cold, and I was in the building where my office is. I passed this guy, and as we passed each other he never

looked at me, but I heard all these things [coming out of his mouth]
and he looked at me and called me a "boy" in a very derogatory
way. I mean, everything about him was meant to incite a situation
and this is what a lot of students had said. I think he thought I was
a student. He recognized me in a coat and a tie, but he postured
himself as though he had a weapon with him. Of course, you know,
this guy is even bigger than me. Huge guy, looks like he should be
on somebody's football team, and it was one of these situations I
knew. I mean, it was bad; it was wrong; it was not even worth confronting because it would have been a no win situation in terms of
we were the only two there. There would have been no witnesses,
so I immediately went over to the police department and found out
all this other stuff and launched an investigation [against] him.

An interviewee who worked at an HBCU said that although he
had not experienced racism from students, he noticed that some of
the Black students at his institution tended to display racism toward
White students. He said, "Most of the racism comes from students.
The Black students don't want the White students at school. The
school is 85 percent Black, 14 percent White, and one percent other."

A professor in Maryland questioned whether or not students' reac-
tions to her and their evaluations of her teaching were based on her
race. During her interview, she described how students' attitudes can
affect tenure decisions:

I've experienced one major incident in particular. It's one of those
things where you don't know to what degree race played into this,
but it was with our Faculty Affairs Committee. That's where we
send our reviews. We get reviewed in our first year, . . . after our first
semester, then we get reviewed after our second year, then after our
fourth year, and then they make tenure decisions. So, my first semester here was very difficult because of issues with students and
racial issues in terms of how students reacted to me. . . . What I got
from the Faculty Affairs Committee, at least the way that I felt after
dealing with them, was that I was kind of making this all up, and it
was all in my head and really I just needed to get my act together,

not something necessarily that [students] were intentionally doing or whatever. But I believed . . . that it was influenced by race. But again, it's one of those things that's hard to pinpoint.

Racism from Faculty Colleagues

Whereas 17 percent of the faculty who completed the questionnaire said they had never experienced cultural insensitivity from their faculty colleagues, 27 percent said they had never experienced racism from their faculty colleagues. Conversely, 70 percent said they had. Three predictors surfaced through regression analysis. These predictors revealed that faculty who said they had never experienced racism from colleagues had never experienced cultural insensitivity from their colleagues, had never experienced cultural insensitivity from their students, and were more likely than others to say the racial climate at work had not caused stress for them.

During the interview phase of the study, several interesting details related to racism from colleagues emerged. Some of the examples pertained to comments from colleagues that were perceived to be racist; other pertained to behaviors. For example, one professor described an incident in which a colleague offended her. She explained:

Now, there was one instance that . . . perhaps I could see racism in. I would call it "latent racism." . . . I graduated from Howard University School of Law, but in my faculty handbook, for some reason, Harvard University [was written]. I had a faculty member who I didn't know very well come up to me at a Christmas party and say, "Oh, I'm so proud of you. I didn't know you graduated from Harvard." So I said, "No, I didn't graduate from Harvard. I graduated from Howard University School of Law in Washington, D.C." He said, "Well, in the faculty handbook they had you listed as Harvard." I never even read [the faculty handbook] about anybody else, let alone [about myself]. And so, by the next day of school, he had called OIT which is our computer programming [office] which puts out the faculty handbook to let them know that they had made a mistake. I thought about it because he's just another faculty member, just as I am. At the time, I think I was the only Black person, so I was wondering what made him look up my credentials even, to the point that at a party, he wanted to discuss them with me, and before I could even look it up to see if he was correct, he felt the need to have it corrected. Did he go to anybody else and say, "Did you go to the University of Florida?" So I felt [there was] latent racism there.

Racism from Immediate Supervisors

Thirty-eighty percent of the faculty who completed the questionnaire said they had never experienced cultural insensitivity from their department chair or dean at their current institution. Forty-seven percent said they had never experienced racism from their chair or dean, but more than half said they had. A stepwise multiple regression equation produced several predictors of how faculty responded. Faculty who had never experienced cultural insensitivity or racism from non-chair or non-dean administrators, their colleagues, or their students were unlikely to have experienced racism from their immediate supervisor. The same was true of faculty who had never felt undermined by their colleagues.

Racism from Non–Department Chair and Non-Dean Administrators

As we reported in the previous chapter, 30 percent of the faculty who completed the questionnaire said they had never experienced cultural insensitivity from any non–department chair or non-dean administrator. Forty percent said they had never experienced racism from a non-chair or non-dean administrator, but nearly 60 percent said they had. Most of the stepwise multiple regression results that we presented previously in this chapter and in chapter 5 were similar in this case. Two less frequently cited predictors indicated that faculty who had never felt that any administrator was trying to undermine them at their current institution, and faculty who felt that their contributions were valued by their colleagues, department chair, and dean were more likely to say they had never experienced racism from a non-chair or non-dean administrator.

Several of the interviewees discussed reasons why they perceived administrators to be racist or not. Some comments suggest that a lack of action by administrators when action is warranted can be perceived as "racism by omission." For example, a professor who taught in the East said that questionable behavior often surfaced from staff and administrators as a result of the combination of her race and youthful look. She explained:

> No matter how many times I say I'm a faculty member to staff, it still doesn't sink into people's heads. I have difficulty getting in people's heads that I am a faculty member in terms of staff and administration. A part of that is also because I'm very young looking, but that in combination with my race makes it difficult. You know, I'll say, "Oh yeah, I'm a faculty member at such and such." [Yet] I'll always get, "I'm sorry, you can't come in here; it's for faculty only." It's kind of hard to separate the race and age issue. I haven't really experienced the blatant things, just everyday kind of very subtle things that aren't really intentional.

Another professor also spoke about subtle versus overt racism, which she had experienced "very covertly, not in my face." She said, "I'm not a person that you would just confront. The vice president sees me as a menace [but] I'm somewhat sheltered from her. Because I have a huge responsibility, my site supervisor shields me from her, because it is known that anybody that she perceives as a threat can be replaced." (See table 6.1 for a summary of the questionnaire results about the faculty's experiences with racism.)

Evaluations

In trying to ascertain the role of the evaluation process in the job satisfaction of Black faculty, we gave them opportunities to describe related experiences, primarily via the questionnaire. Although faculty,

TABLE 6.1
Faculty's Experiences with Racism by Percentage

Statement	Agree	Disagree
At my current institution, I have never experienced any racism from my faculty colleagues.	27	70
At my current institution, I have never experienced any racism from my immediate supervisor, such as my department chair or dean.	47	51
At my current institution, I have never experienced any racism from any non-chair or non-dean administrator.	40	57
At my current institution, I have never experienced any racism from any of my students.	23	74
Racism is uncommon at my institution.	15	84
The racial climate at my institution does not affect my job satisfaction.	32	67
The racial climate at my institution has not caused stress for me.	33	66

$N = 136$
Note: The difference in percentage totals that are less than 100 can be explained by the number of participants who failed to respond to certain statements.

including non-Blacks, can receive unfair evaluations for a number of reasons, for faculty of color, unfair evaluations often stem from racism. We specifically wanted to know if the participants in our study had received unfair evaluations at their current institution. Three questionnaire items pertained to unfair evaluations: from students, immediate supervisors, and colleagues (see table 6.2). Then, we asked participants to describe how the evaluations affected them.

Twenty-three percent of the questionnaire respondents said they had never received unfair teaching evaluations from their students. Twenty-four percent said they had, but it was rare, and 38 percent said they had received unfair evaluations from students more frequently. Overall, more than 60 percent of the faculty said they had received

TABLE 6.2
Faculty's Experiences with Unfair Evaluations by Percentage

Statement	Never	Rarely	Frequently
I have received unfair evaluations from students.	23	24	38
I have received unfair evaluations from colleagues.	36	38	12
I have received unfair evaluations from an immediate supervisor.	41	29	15

$N = 136$
Note: The difference in percentage totals that are less than 100 can be explained by the number of participants who failed to respond to certain statements.

unfair evaluations from students. This is very important to note since student evaluations usually carry a lot of weight when faculty are evaluated for tenure and promotion, especially at teaching universities. Therefore, negative and unfair evaluations could very well determine whether an untenured faculty member is permitted to remain at an institution.

Bivariate correlation analysis revealed that faculty who said they experienced racism or cultural insensitivity at their institution, faculty who said that the racial climate had caused stress for them, and those who said the racial climate had affected their job satisfaction were more likely than those who did not to say they had received unfair teaching evaluations from students. These faculty were also less likely to feel valued at their institutions.

Nearly 40 percent of the questionnaire respondents said they had never received unfair periodic evaluations from their colleagues. Thirty-eight percent said they had, but it was rare, and 12 percent said that it had occurred more frequently. Therefore, half of the respondents said they had received unfair evaluations from colleagues. Faculty who said they had been evaluated unfairly by their colleagues were more likely than others to say the racial climate at work had been stressful for them and that they were dissatisfied with the way in which their department chair or dean had handled most culturally or racially sensitive issues that affected them.

Forty-one percent of the questionnaire respondents said they had never received unfair periodic evaluations from their department chair or dean. Nearly 30 percent said they had, but it was rare, and 15 percent said they had received them more frequently. Through bivariate correlation analysis, we learned that in addition to saying that racism and cultural insensitivity were common at their institution, faculty who said they had been unfairly evaluated by their immediate supervisor were also more likely to say that the racial climate at work had been stressful for them and had affected their job satisfaction. Moreover, these faculty tended to believe that their colleagues, chair, and dean did not value their contributions. Three other factors differentiated this group from faculty who said they had not been unfairly evaluated by their immediate supervisor: (1) they were more likely to state that they had not become adept at handling racially or culturally challenging situations at work, (2) they were more likely to be dissatisfied about how they had handled most culturally or racially sensitive incidents that affected them personally at work, and (3) they tended to be dissatisfied with how their immediate supervisor had handled most of these situations.

How Cultural Insensitivity and Racism Were Handled

Five questionnaire items permitted participants to explain how they personally handled cultural insensitivity and racism at their institution (if they existed) and whether or not they were satisfied with how their immediate supervisor handled these problems (see table 6.3). Twelve percent of the questionnaire respondents said that when a racially or culturally challenging situation occurred at work, they ignored the situation. Bivariate correlation analysis revealed that the faculty who were most likely to ignore such situations were more likely to state that they had felt devalued by their department chair, dean, and colleagues, and that they had been verbally disrespected by a university

TABLE 6.3
Questionnaire Results Pertaining to How Racism and Cultural Insensitivity Were Handled by Percentage

Statement	Agree	Disagree
I have become adept at handling racially or culturally challenging situations at work.	75	22
When a racially or culturally challenging situation occurs at work, I ignore the situation.	12	83
I am satisfied with the way in which I have handled most culturally and/or racially sensitive situations that affected me personally at my institution.	68	29
I am satisfied with the way in which my immediate supervisor has handled most culturally and/or racially sensitive incidents that affected me at my institution.	43	54
When a racially or culturally challenging situation occurs at work, I voice my displeasure to my colleagues, chair, and/or dean.	72	25

$N = 136$
Note: The difference in percentage totals that are less than 100 can be explained by the number of participants who failed to respond to certain statements.

administrator. However, they were also likely to say they were satisfied with the way in which they (the faculty members) handled most culturally and/or racially sensitive incidents that had affected them at their current institution.

An interviewee told an interesting story about an incident that troubled her, yet she chose to ignore it. She said:

> One of my colleagues is originally from Greece and she told a story about seeing a Black person, an African exchange student, for the first time [when she was a child]. She and her friend decided that if they walked and didn't look at this man, he wouldn't eat them. She was telling me this story in terms of this is what she thought at eight or 10 years old. And you know, it was just sort of a hurtful story, but I just sort of smiled and nodded along with the other people at

the table, because I had to realize that what she didn't know was that we don't eat people. . . . But just the idea that she felt she could tell this story, my God! I didn't dwell on it. I moved on. I would never approach her about it, because that's not the basis of our relationship.

I do ignore [racist and culturally sensitive situations] and it's the best response, because I need to do my job. It [not ignoring such situations] just becomes too distracting and I work with so many minority students that I've decided that it is a low priority. I'm West Indian and at the end of the day, that's what saves me. . . . We always exercised what we called our "moral superiority." We know the difference between right and wrong, and we just feel it's beneath us to let this kind of irrational behavior affect our lives, the quality of our lives.

Whereas 12 percent of the questionnaire respondents said they chose to ignore racist and culturally insensitive behavior at work, 72 percent said that when a racially or culturally challenging situation occurred at work, they voiced their displeasure to their colleagues, chair, and/or dean. Through bivariate correlation analysis, we learned that "vocal" faculty were more likely than others to say they had felt supported and respected by (non-chair and non-dean) administrators and they felt valued at their institution.

Several interviewees provided additional information about this topic. For example, a male professor said that he addressed racism and cultural insensitivity through "my mode of communication. Usually, I'm not trying to be defensive. However, I am letting them know how I feel. If I don't agree, I give my rationale as to why I disagree. Usually, it's not what a person says, but how they say it."

In describing how she handled a racially challenging situation, another professor said, "I feel that I kept a professional perspective, but also conveyed a message related to the issue. I always try to make situations a teaching experience. I put the ownership of responsibility on them. I allow them to take ownership of the situation, thereby, not allowing a situation to become out of control and overwhelming."

Another interviewee said, "I don't ignore it. If it happens or I see it, I usually speak about it or react in some way to it." A professor who was cautioned about being too vocal before receiving tenure said, "I don't bite my tongue. However, I was not tenured and someone said I was very vocal and that I should be careful. My response was that I would not be censored, tenured or not."

One interviewee spoke emphatically about the danger of ignoring racially and culturally sensitive issues by explaining, "I don't ignore it; I try to respond to it. The reason that I respond is because I feel like if I don't respond, it helps to promote their desire or to continue with it. I feel like by responding, I can somewhat nip it in the bud to a degree. I won't get *that* question from *that* person again, but I will get it again. I won't get *that* comment from *that* person again, but I will get it again."

Another interviewee who was equally emphatic said, "I never ignore any racial anything that comes across my desk. No, I certainly would never do that. In fact, if I heard something from students or other colleagues on any level, I would be the one to walk them over to the Dean of Students' office or the campus police department to deal with the situation."

Nearly 70 percent of the faculty said they were satisfied with how they had personally handled most culturally and/or racially sensitive incidents that affected them at their institution, and 75 percent said they had actually become "adept" at handling racially or culturally challenging situations at work. For example, one interviewee stated, "I've learned to pick my battles and prioritize what's really important to me." A professor in North Carolina attributed his adeptness to his own prior experiences and his institution's openness about issues related to diversity. He explained:

> I came here with experience in dealing with issues of training in diversity. . . . I think I've been in such a good situation because at this university, they were pretty open, or let's say I made them become open—to open the eyes of the university. So, in terms of intol-

erance on any level, I've certainly been a part of [addressing] that. It has also helped me to do more in terms of training and also better prepared me as to how to respond to situations and the way to confront things. I have actually challenged the university. So now, we have become more proactive than reactive when we have situations. When we hear things, we need to begin looking into these situations early before something explodes or becomes very explosive.

Another interviewee said:

I feel satisfied with the way I've handled the issues that I've dealt with because it's reflective of who I am as a person. It's reflective of my values and whom I see myself as. I feel like my parents, my grandparents, my son, and my family members would say, "You know what? He did so good by his name." So you know, I'm happy with what I've done because I think it's representative of who I am as a person.

A professor who explained why she chose to act on some situations and yet ignore others said:

There have been a few incidents that I have ignored. For the most part, it doesn't hurt me and I choose to ignore it because it would serve no purpose to address it. However, if I were being passed over for a promotion and I felt it was attributed to race, than I'd address it. Further, I choose not to be offensive because it's not going to change their behavior. Although I'll admit that some things are inadvertent, I also realize that others are involuntary. For instance, when people see someone who is very large, they turn around and look, yet if the person stopped and challenged that, they would be doing that all day long.

In explaining how each particular situation can determine how it might be handled, another interviewee remarked:

It all just depends on the situation. Things that are innocent and subtle and in passing you know, where I'm just left thinking, "Was that about this?" or you know, "What was that about?" I might just let it go. Other things, certainly things that are subtle, I tend to want to address in some format, actually sometimes to my detriment. There are some times when I just need to be quiet and I have a hard time not telling people how I feel about something and . . . it just really depends on what form it comes in. But with things that are more blatant and direct, I have a tendency to want to address it in some way, shape, or form.

The things that I've experienced have not been that cut and dried necessarily. . . . For example, initially, when I went through this experience in my first semester, and then I had this negative experience with the Faculty Affairs Committee, who like I said, kind of approached me as, "Well, this is all in your head," the chair of my department advised me to let it go. Later on, I decided not to, that I really just couldn't let it go, and I expressed my feelings to both her and to the members of the Faculty Affairs Committee. Now, I'm happy that I did that, but it didn't have [a] positive outcome. It wasn't like it got into their heads. I feel good about the way I handled that, but it didn't necessarily result in a light bulb going off.

Whereas nearly 70 percent of the faculty who completed the questionnaire said they were satisfied with the way they handled racially and culturally challenging situations, only 43 percent said they were satisfied with how their immediate supervisor had handled such situations. Faculty who had not experienced racism or cultural insensitivity and who felt valued and supported at their institutions were more likely than others to be satisfied with how their immediate supervisor handled related situations. Conversely, faculty who felt devalued, marginalized, had been verbally disrespected, and those who had received unfair teaching evaluations were less likely to be satisfied with how their immediate supervisor responded.

One interviewee explained, "Fortunately, for me, I have never had to be in that situation, but I feel very confident that if a culturally sensitive situation of any sort on any level occurred, my supervisor would be very supportive of me because there is trust there in terms of my credibility, and in terms of my ability to be open and fair."

Another interviewee expressed ambivalence, stating, "I have mixed perceptions as to how my supervisor handles issues that I consider to be discriminatory. . . . On one hand, my supervisor attempts to understand and see things from my perspective, but on the other hand, it's like 50–50. All I can say is, 'I don't think my supervisor gets it. I don't think that it's possible for this person to get it.' I think it's inherent to who they are as a culture and some of it, they'll never get."

However, a professor who was pleased when asked to find solutions to a racially challenging situation that he had brought to his supervisor's attention, remarked, "I think he took the appropriate action because he came to me to help him resolve it. He trusted me and sought my advice. I've also done some prep work with him, on situations that might occur. We work together really [well] and it's really an unusual dynamic."

Did the Racial Climate at Work Affect the Participants' Job Satisfaction and Stress Levels?

Two questionnaire items asked participants to state whether or not the racial climate at their institution affected their job satisfaction or caused stress for them (see table 6.1). Several interviewees also commented on these topics.

One-third of the questionnaire respondents said the racial climate at their institution had not caused stress for them, but two-thirds said it had. Through bivariate correlation analysis, we learned several pertinent details. First, we learned that faculty who had never experienced any racism or cultural insensitivity at work and those who worked at institutions at which cultural insensitivity and racism were uncommon were likely to say the racial climate at work had not caused stress for them. Second, we learned that faculty who felt that racist and culturally challenging situations were handled appropriately and who felt supported and valued also tended to say it had not caused stress for them. Conversely, faculty who felt marginalized, had received unfair evaluations, had experienced professional jealousy, who said that their colleagues, chair, dean, and other administrators' devaluation of them was racially motivated, and those who believed their scholarship was devalued by their colleagues and their immediate supervisor were more likely to say the racial climate had caused stress for them.

Comments from interviewees gave us additional information about the link between stress and an institution's racial climate. For example, in explaining why the racial climate at work was not stressful for him, a male professor said, "I don't have a problem related to the racial climate; it's more a problem of personality for me than race." Another interviewee who agreed that the racial climate was not stressful remarked:

> I cannot think of any time where I . . . have felt stressed or unsatisfied [at this university] because of any racial incident or policy. . . . I have felt very satisfied being here, given the university's position and formal position on social justice. We have a very strong social justice policy within the university and it is that social justice policy that basically attracted me to the university. So if anything, [my] satisfaction [level] is positive.

An interviewee who said that some of her colleagues' assumptions caused stress for her explained:

> Yes, it does cause me stress. In the process of collecting data I was working with working-class and middle-class African American families, and [another] researcher just assumed that because we were Black in color, that it would be easy and smooth sailing for me, and it wasn't. I represented the university, so I had to deal with the same problems that any researcher did, and they just didn't seem to understand that. They just assumed that because I was Black that I should be able to collect the data from Black families. Not the case at all.

Whereas 66 percent of the questionnaire respondents said the racial climate at their institution had caused stress for them, 67 percent said that it had actually affected their job satisfaction to some degree. Most of the same factors that were correlated with whether or not the racial climate had been stressful for them were correlated with their responses about the effect of the racial climate on their job satisfaction. However, there were some differences, such as faculty were more likely to say the racial climate had not affected their job satisfaction if they had other Black colleagues in their department. Furthermore, although faculty who said they had received unfair evaluations from students, colleagues, and administrators were more likely to say the racial climate at their institution had caused stress for them, some respondents said that receiving unfair evaluations had even affected their job satisfaction enough to warrant leaving their institution.

Several interviewees explained why the racial climate at their institution had or had not affected their job satisfaction. For instance, one professor said that her attitude and handling of culturally challenging situations were the main reasons why the racial climate had not affected her job satisfaction. She explained, "No, racism isn't an issue for me. It hasn't kept me from my job or kept me from doing anything. I'll tell them when they are outside the boundaries. I make it a learning experience. I tell them, 'Let's look at this.' They listen and learn."

Another professor remarked, "No, the climate hasn't been that bad. The mission and the climate at the school are about diversity and sensitivity, however, we do have our moments." Another professor who was pleased with the overall racial climate stated:

> It certainly has not caused me any job dissatisfaction because I think that our racial climate has been . . . I think that they're very fortunate or maybe just a lot of things have not been reported. But I've had no hardships [at] the university, because like I said, "I can't really even cite an example." I've been pretty pleased in terms of how I've felt when the university was trying to deal with any acts of intolerance that came across my desk. Again, with the exception of that one case that I cited earlier, but I understood, you know, in

terms of [the] law, the procedure that they had to take, and I guess I was a little more forceful with them with that situation. My satisfaction has been pretty good in terms of the racial climate.

A professor who spoke about the impact of the city's diversity and the diversity at her institution on her job satisfaction said:

It probably has affected my job satisfaction. . . . I'm on a very diverse campus. As a matter of fact, it's a Catholic institution, and one of its pillars is that of diversity, and it's in the Miami area. You know the diversity we have here. Plus, this university is really a complement of Miami, and I have had some really positive [experiences with] the mixture of the races. I work with an Anglo lady and a Hispanic lady and because of our uniqueness, we've kind of formed a consultant company called "Diversity, Inc." where we prepare seminars and we take it out into the community, unemployment places, and the like, and it's really very beneficial.

Conversely, unlike the aforementioned professor, several interviewees said that the lack of diversity at their institution, specifically the small number of Black faculty, had an impact on the racial climate and had a negative effect on their job satisfaction.

Summary

The results that we presented in this chapter reveal that although many individuals who work at postsecondary institutions continue to believe that racism no longer exists in American society, it remains alive in the Academy (Baez & Centra, 1995; Bell, 1994; Gregory, 1995; Jayate, 2002; Perna, 2002; Toth 2002b; Turner & Myers, 2000; White & Siwatu, 2002). Like Turner and Myers (2000) who said, "faculty of color we interviewed offer convincing testimony of pervasive racial and ethnic bias in the academic workplace," (p. 143), we found that the majority of participants in our study said they had been subjected to racism from students and their colleagues. Moreover, nearly 60 percent had experienced it from one or more university-level administrators and more than half had experienced it from their immediate supervisor. Additionally, two-thirds of the faculty said that the racial climate at their institution had caused stress for them and nearly 70 percent said that it had affected their job satisfaction.

As researchers and African American faculty, it is our opinion that the solutions are obvious. The Academy must become proactive in acknowledging that racism exists in higher education. This topic must no longer be perceived as one of the "elephants" that continues to sit in the living room but that is ignored by many in the Academy. In addition to acknowledging its existence, the Academy must identify racism's many guises—including the covert forms of racism that often hide behind a liberal, social justice agenda (Jones, 2002; Thompson, 2004b). Leaders in postsecondary institutions must seek the input of Black and non-Black administrators, faculty, staff, and students in developing an action plan (Smith, 1995). This input is clearly needed because more than half of the participants in our study were dissatisfied with how their immediate supervisor had handled racially sensitive incidents.

The fact that 84 percent of the participants in our study said that cultural insensitivity was common at their institution and 84 percent said that racism was common should set off alarm bells at institutions that are seriously committed to improving Black faculty retention rates. These results reveal that many Black faculty truly view and experience life in the Academy very differently from their White colleagues and supervisors (Bell, 1994; Gregory, 1995; Jarmon, 2001; Jones, 2002; Mabokela & Green, 2001; Moses, 1989), especially colleagues and administrators who remain in denial about the existence of racism. This denial may contribute to Black faculty dissatisfaction. Because many Black faculty had experienced racism from students, colleagues, and administrators, there is clearly a need for leaders in postsecondary institutions to address these problems. The following story underscores the message that we concluded the last chapter with and that we want to repeat as we conclude this one: "Leadership sets the tone for what is acceptable and unacceptable in organizations."

In October 2004, a White graduate student who was enrolled in a class taught by one of us, shared a story with this author that is pertinent to the findings that we presented in this chapter and the message that we seek to emphasize. During the previous week, the student had e-mailed the author saying that she would have to miss class because of a family crisis. When she came to class a week later, the author asked how she and her family were doing. The student explained that her absence had not been caused by a crisis in the traditional sense of the word, but by a series of upsetting incidents involving her four-year-old daughter and her preschool classmates.

The director of the preschool had summoned all of the parents to an emergency meeting to express her displeasure over the fact that all of the preschoolers had turned against the only two African American children at the school. Many of the children, including the African Americans, had been enrolled in the school since they were infants. They had shared secrets with one another, played together, and cried together. However, during 2004, the non-Black children had systematically begun to exclude the African Americans from activities and games. When one class activity required the children to hold hands with each other, the graduate student's four-year-old daughter became upset about having to hold the little Black boy's hand. So, she pulled her shirt sleeve over her hand to avoid touching him. The little Black girl in the class was only permitted to have "group insider status" when she wore her hair a certain way—the way that the non-Black girls in the class had told her was the appropriate style.

As the author listened to the graduate student describe these events, she felt overwhelming sadness for the little Black preschoolers who were experiencing racism at such an early age. If racism can have dramatic consequences for adults and even lead to high blood pressure and other medical problems as some researchers contend, how much more difficult must it be for small children to handle, she wondered? However, two other components of the story gave the author a glimmer of hope that penetrated her sadness over the African American children's dilemma. First, both the White graduate student and her husband, a Mexican American, became outraged and proactive when they learned what was happening at the school. They made it clear to their daughter that her behavior and that of her classmates was not only inappropriate, but they would not tolerate such conduct. The child's father was even more upset, because as a member of a historically oppressed group, he had experienced racism firsthand. Both he and his wife shared "teachable moment" stories with their daughter and reminded her that she and the African American boy used to be close friends who had shared many positive experiences.

The second glimmer of hope came from the graduate student's description of the preschool director's behavior. When she learned what the children were doing, the director did not ignore the situation, she did not blame the victims, and she did not accuse them of overreacting or imagining things. In other words, she was not in denial, as many ineffective leaders of organizations and institutions are. Instead, as the person in charge, the director set the tone that prevented the situation from escalating. Believing that the Black children had been wronged, she summoned all of the parents to the school, informed them of what had been happening, said the racist behavior was unacceptable, and discussed an action plan with them. One of the components of this action plan was that the curriculum would become more multicultural, in order to teach the children to value and appreciate other groups. The director was also holding the parents accountable for doing their part to ensure that the racist behavior would cease. Her actions sent a clear message to students, teachers, and parents that racism would not be tolerated at the school. This message was, undoubtedly, validating and reassuring to the Black children and their parents.

Since the author first heard this story, she has often wondered what would happen if when faced with allegations of racism and cultural insensitivity, leaders in postsecondary institutions became as vigilant and proactive as the preschool director did. In other words, what would happen if they became the "connective leaders" that Lipman-Blumen (1998) described? According to Lipman-Blumen, connective leaders build "connections among diverse, often contentious groups" (p. 50). Consequently, they reap rewards. The payoffs of such successful leadership result in an institutional or organizational climate where people are committed to their work and "where creativity and innovation can grow, where people feel a sense of meaning in their lives, and where their dedication to a cause larger than themselves ennobles and enables others" (p. 53). However, another benefit of connective leadership is an institutional climate in which "diversity and interdependence potentiate one another" (p. 53). Tony Brown (1995) spoke directly about the role of leaders in eliminating racism. He stated, "The truth is that efficient management will eliminate the impact of personal racism. Racism will be viewed as an economic liability in a truly culturally diverse environment—if goals are clearly articulated, and incentives and penalties are linked to performance and corporate culture" (p. 216).

It is our hope that like the aforementioned preschool director, leaders in postsecondary institutions will rise to the challenge of becoming the types of leaders that Lipman-Blumen (1998) and Tony Brown (1995) described as being instrumental in improving organizational and institutional climates and creating fully inclusive institutions. In the next chapter, "The Bright Side of the Academy," we will return to the topic of racism once again, as an indicator of how strongly connected it is to Black faculty dissatisfaction in the Academy. We will share specific recommendations from the participants in our study about how leaders can improve the racial climate in the Academy, and in the conclusion of this book, we will say more about the crucial role leaders can play in improving postsecondary institutions.

7

THE BRIGHT SIDE OF
THE ACADEMY

Sources of Satisfaction and
Recommendations from Black Faculty

IN APRIL 2004, after we (the authors) gave a presentation on "Increasing Black Faculty Satisfaction" at the American Educational Research Association's Annual Conference in San Diego, we had a lengthy conversation that disturbed us with a young African American professor who had attended our presentation. Although we have no idea of whether or not her story is common, we do believe that it underscores the need for the Academy to work harder at retaining Black faculty.

At the time when we met her, she was in her twenties, single, and a tenure-track professor at a PWI in South Carolina. She was attractive, articulate, and amiable. On the surface, she appeared to be what many African American graduate students, newly minted PhDs, and unemployed faculty dream of: successful and in possession of a coveted tenure-track position at a respected university. Moreover, she told us that during her own graduate studies she had received excellent mentoring and thought she had been well prepared for the challenges of the Academy. This preparation included frank discussions about the politics of higher education—politics that, in our opinion (as we mentioned previously), can become just as pernicious as those of the most ruthless and cutthroat organizations in U.S. society.

So, it would have seemed that this young Black professor was destined for professorial success, especially since her university had also asked a senior professor to mentor her when she arrived. The reality, however, was different, and as she shared her story, we became increasingly troubled. While it was true that she had accomplished a noteworthy feat in attaining a tenure-track position at this university, complete with a "seasoned" mentor, at the end of her first year in the professoriate, she had decided that a career in higher education was not for her. In other words, she had not just decided to leave that particular institution, but had decided to quit the Academy completely.

We were appalled and told her so. We told her that she had a professional obligation not to quit. We told her that she must honor the legacy of her predecessors: African Americans like W. E. B. DuBois, E. Franklin Frazier, Charles Johnson, Carter G. Woodson, and numerous other individuals who had struggled with racism, oppression, and other barriers, yet had paved the way for African Americans like herself. But no amount of coaxing, cajoling, or guilt-trip-inducing messages could change her mind. She was resolute—undeterred in her decision to leave the Academy.

As she continued to speak candidly about her decision, we slowly began to understand her rationale. Although she appeared to have a great job, the institutional portrait that she painted for us captured a lonely, isolated journey that had a long history. When she and another young African American woman were hired at this university, there was only one other African American professor in the entire university, a woman who had been there for twenty years. However, both of the new assistant professors were assigned to work with White mentors. The young woman who shared her story with us said that her mentor had tried very hard to do a good job, but their different academic fields made connecting with each other somewhat difficult. Her colleague, the other young African American woman who was hired at the same time, did not fare as well. "They assigned her to a mentor who doesn't even like Black people," the young professor told us.

The institutional portrait that emerged from her description was one of a university that proclaimed loudly that it was serious about diversifying the faculty. In practice, another message surfaced. "It's in a hick town," she told us. "We got no support from the university. A lot of the attitudes and clichés that we heard made us feel very unwelcome. They say they want diversity, but when the people come, it's a different story." That "story" included the fact that the young professors were subjected to rudeness from secretaries, who evidently wanted them to know that in spite of their doctorates, they were still inferior to them. She concluded by telling us, "They're trying to get more Black professors, but they can't keep them." Consequently, one month later, she planned to leave this university and the Academy completely, without a backward glance. Her goal was to become a preschool teacher. When we told her that she might appear to be overqualified as a preschool teacher with a doctorate, she replied that she didn't care. In her opinion, few things could compare to the politics, racism, and coldness that she had experienced during her one-year stint as a tenure-track professor at a university that only appeared to want African American faculty as tokens, but whose institutional climate and norms constantly told her that she was not welcome.

Since then, we have pondered this story often. Despite the fact that we wished she had merely decided to go elsewhere, we ultimately understood her decision to leave. In fact, throughout this book thus far, we have attempted to identify factors that prompt Black faculty to become dissatisfied enough to leave postsecondary institutions. Most of these factors were evident in this young professor's case. She had experienced racism. She worked at an institution where racism and cultural insensitivity were common. She had been repeatedly disrespected, and although university officials had assigned her to a mentor, she still felt that, overall, the work environment was nonsupportive.

Turner and Myers (2000) cited a number of factors that contributed to the decision to remain in the Academy by the faculty of color that they studied. They wrote, "intellectual challenge, freedom to pursue research interests, and the opportunity to promote racial/ethnic understanding" (p. 143) were some of the professional rewards that compelled them to stay. Personal rewards that motivated faculty of color to stay included their satisfaction with teaching, having mentors, having supportive administrators, collegiality, and their interactions with other faculty of color. In the case of the young African American professor from South Carolina whom we met, most, if not all, of these personal and professional rewards were lacking at her institution. This lack of personal and professional rewards became the catalyst that prompted her to leave the Academy entirely.

In a final attempt to help leaders in the Academy ascertain how best to retain Black faculty, in this chapter we look at the "bright side of the Academy," the aspects of "life" in postsecondary institutions that are most rewarding to Black faculty and we share the recommendations that the participants in our study made. We hope that leaders in the Academy who are sincere about increasing Black faculty satisfaction and, thereby, retention rates, will use this information to prevent other faculty from becoming disillusioned enough to become preschool teachers, at a time when Black faculty are desperately needed in many PWIs. We do so by answering three questions: (1) Which of their professional responsibilities were most important to the Black faculty who participated in our study? (2) What were the most rewarding aspects of "life" in the Academy for them? and (3) What were their recommendations about how the Academy can increase the job satisfaction of Black faculty?

The Participants' Most Important Professional Responsibilities

The faculty who completed the questionnaire were asked to identify which of their professional responsibilities were most important to them from a list of six options (see table 7.1) and they could write in other responsibilities. Teaching emerged as the most frequently cited most important professional responsibility. Nearly half of the faculty

TABLE 7.1
Participants' Most Important Professional Responsibilities

Responsibility	Percent Who Ranked It as the Single Most Important	Percent Who Ranked It as One of the Three Most Important
Teaching	47	74
Research	27	58
Mentoring	15	57
Writing	11	40
Presenting	7	25
Community service	6	38
Other	4	5

$N = 136$
Note: Percentage totals exceed 100 because some respondents ranked more than one questionnaire option as their single most important responsibility.

ranked it as the most important, and more than 70 percent ranked it as one of their three most important professional responsibilities. Female faculty were more likely than males to say that teaching was their most important professional responsibility. Second, faculty who taught at community colleges and faculty at comprehensive non–research universities were more likely than those at research universities to rank teaching as their most important professional duty.

Conducting research emerged as the second most frequently cited professional duty. More than a quarter of the faculty ranked it as the most important, and nearly 60 percent ranked it as one of their top three most important duties. Faculty at research universities were more likely than others to rank conducting research as one of their most important professional duties. These faculty were also more likely to rank writing as one of their most important professional responsibilities but unlikely to place a high priority on performing community service or on teaching as professional duties. Another finding indicated that faculty who ranked conducting research as one of their most important professional duties had a greater probability of saying they had not experienced racism from their faculty colleagues and from university administrators.

Fifteen percent of the questionnaire respondents ranked mentoring as their most important professional responsibility and nearly 60 percent ranked it as one of their top three. These professors were more likely than others to also select performing community service as one of their most important duties.

Writing, giving presentations, and performing community service were the three professional responsibilities that few professors ranked as their single most important professional duty. However, one-fourth or more of the faculty ranked these responsibilities as one of their top three most important obligations.

What Matters to Black Faculty? The Most Rewarding Aspects of "Life" in the Academy for the Participants

As in the case of identifying the most difficult aspects of their work at their current institution (see table 1.5), faculty could also select from a list of thirteen options (see table 7.2) in order to identify the aspects of their job that were most rewarding. They also had the option of specifying "other" aspects. The data revealed that their most important professional obligations (as described in the previous section) were not necessarily the aspects of their jobs that they found to be the most rewarding.

As table 1.5 indicated, about one-fifth of the questionnaire respondents said that mentoring students of color was one of the top five most difficult aspects of their job and 43 percent said it was one of the top ten. Moreover, only 15 percent of the faculty ranked mentoring as their single most important professional obligation. In spite of this, nearly 60 percent ranked mentoring students of color as one of the top five most rewarding aspects of their job, and nearly 70 percent ranked it as one of the ten most rewarding aspects. The faculty who were most likely to select mentoring as one of the most rewarding aspects of their job tended to be satisfied enough to remain at their institution and they believed that their professional success was important to their colleagues, chair, and dean.

TABLE 7.2
What Matters to Black Faculty? The Most Rewarding Aspects of "Life"
in the Academy for the Study's Participants

Aspect	Percent Who Ranked It as One of the Top Five	Percent Who Ranked It as One of the Top Ten
Mentoring students of color	57	69
Your research	52	62
Community service work	41	60
Course preparation	38	62
Interpersonal relations with colleagues	38	60
Support from other African Americans	33	56
Teaching load	32	54
Support from other colleagues of color	28	54
Collegial relations with chair or dean	25	40
Administrative support	24	54
Number of faculty of color	24	44
Committee work	21	47
Racial climate	13	36
Other	5	5

$N = 136$

Similar contrasts between what faculty deemed as the most important aspects rather than the most rewarding aspects of their job emerged in other areas. For example, although only 27 percent of the faculty said that conducting research was their single most important professional responsibility, more than half ranked it as one of the top five most rewarding aspects of their job. Second, whereas only 6 percent of the faculty said that performing community service was their single most important professional duty, 41 percent ranked it as one of the top five most rewarding aspects of their job.

Two factors pertaining to teaching brought joy to some faculty. Nearly 40 percent enjoyed preparing for their classes enough to cite it as one of the most rewarding aspects of their jobs. Nearly one-third said the teaching load was among the most rewarding aspects.

Once again, race and collegial relations also surfaced as important factors to some faculty. Nearly 40 percent found their interpersonal relations with their colleagues to be one of the top five most gratifying aspects of their job. One-third of the faculty said that receiving support from other African Americans was one of the most rewarding aspects of their job. Third, nearly a quarter or more of the faculty said that support from other colleagues of color, collegial relations with their chair or dean, administrative support, and the number of faculty of color were among the top five most rewarding aspects of their job (see table 7.2).

Few faculty found committee work or the racial climate at their institution to be among the five most rewarding aspects of their job. Only a fifth of the faculty said that committee work was one of the most rewarding aspects. However, besides "other" (the write-in option), the least frequently cited most rewarding aspect was the racial climate. Only 13 percent of the faculty indicated that the racial climate at their institution was one of the top five most gratifying aspects of their job. These faculty tended to be tenured, to feel valued at their institution, and to state that they had never experienced cultural insensitivity at work or experienced stress as a result of the racial climate.

Recommendations from the Study's Participants

The faculty in our study also had an opportunity to describe specific ways in which postsecondary institutions can increase Black faculty job satisfaction by responding to a survey question that asked, "What steps can the Academy take to increase African American faculty job satisfaction?" Four blank lines were provided for write-in responses.

Fifty-four percent of the total sample of questionnaire respondents made recommendations. Their recommendations fall into five broad categories: (1) diversity and climate issues, (2) support, (3) professional duties, (4) compensation and other incentives, and (5) other recommendations (see table 7.3).

Diversity and Climate Issues

Sixty percent of the faculty who made recommendations focused on diversity and climate issues. The main themes were:

- Postsecondary institutions should recruit more Black faculty, Black administrators, and Black students.

TABLE 7.3
Participants' Recommendations for Increasing Black Faculty Satisfaction

Suggestions	Percent
Improve the campus climate:	60
—Recruit more Black faculty	
—Improve the racial climate	
—Provide diversity training for all constituents	
Increase support for Black faculty:	43
—Mentoring	
—Value the input, opinions, other contributions, and so forth, of Black faculty	
Professional duties:	19
—Reduce the teaching load	
—Provide assistance with research	
—Reduce the committee workload	
Compensation and other incentives:	10
—Better salaries	
—Equitable pay	
Other suggestions:	8
—Improve tenure and promotion practices	
—Respect community service	
—Respect Black faculty's work with African American students	

$N = 73$

- Institutions must address issues, policies, and practices that make the racial climate unwelcoming and difficult for Black faculty.
- Institutions must do a better job of providing diversity training for all of their constituents.

We have discussed all of these themes in previous chapters and we will revisit them in the following sections.

Recruitment

Numerous professors wrote about the need for postsecondary institutions to recruit and retain more Black faculty. A woman who taught at a public four-year comprehensive university in the Midwest said, "We need to improve in the area of employment. Our campus has only a small African American faculty." A man who taught at a public university in the West said that his university did not actively search for Black faculty. In order to increase Black faculty satisfaction he said that universities must "look for them." In other words, they must earnestly seek to increase the number of Black faculty. Another professor in the West made a similar remark: "Aggressive recruitment is needed and efforts should be made to retain the current African American faculty." A professor who had taught at a private university in the Northeast for several years said, "More people of color are needed to form a critical mass."

Several respondents said that current recruitment practices should be improved. For example, one of the study's participants emphasized that hiring should also target senior professors. He wrote, "Hire more Blacks and associate and full professors who are Black." A woman who had taught at a southeastern public research university for nearly ten years suggested, "Cast the net more broadly when advertising. Diversity requires commitment from the leadership. Cluster hiring." Several other faculty agreed that effective recruitment must be broad. It must include students, administrators, and staff. In other words, increasing Black faculty satisfaction requires the prevalence of "Black faces" at all levels of the Academy, and as one participant stated, "Representation is needed across disciplines." Moreover, when institutions increase the number of Black graduate students they enroll, they increase the probability that a continuous supply of potential Black faculty will be available to eventually enter the professorial pipeline. A male professor in the Midwest put it simply: "Train more African American graduate students. Recruit more African American administrators."

Improving the Racial Climate

Many of the study's participants also stressed that improving Black faculty satisfaction entails improving the racial climate in postsecondary institutions, a topic that we discussed in the previous chapter. In other words, as a woman who had taught at a public university in the West for less than a year stated, institutions must "transform the racist culture on campus." Another professor in the Midwest spoke for many when she wrote, "Change the climate and the community dynamics through commitment." A professor at a small Quaker university in the South said that improving Black faculty satisfaction requires "a culturally diverse environment in which diversity is honored." Moreover, "Acknowledging the existence of racism in higher education institutions," is crucial, according to a male who had taught in the Northwest for less than three years. Another male who had taught in the Northwest for nearly ten years said that racism must be talked about openly.

Several faculty said that the expectations of individuals working in postsecondary institutions must change. For example, a woman who had taught at a private university in the West for less than a year said, institutions must "prove that they value African American faculty by not expecting them to assimilate to the status quo," and they should "commit to different perspectives." A man who had taught for nearly a decade said, "Don't make us have to be all things to all people. Give us credit for doing the stuff Whites won't or can't do."

Strongly worded statements from three participants lent a sense of urgency to the need to improve the racial climate in order to increase Black faculty satisfaction. A woman who had taught at a public research university in the Southwest for ten years urged, "Address racial issues directly. State what they are. Define and act on diversity as an expansion of the present system, not a continuation of it in a different color." A professor who had taught in the Midwest for ten years said that institutions should "Name a respected person or office to monitor the climate and conduct exit interviews." A woman who taught at a public research university in the South was less diplomatic. She said, "Get rid of racism and people who harbor it. That's the only way."

Provide Diversity Training for Everyone

Many of the faculty felt that a comprehensive diversity plan is necessary in order for institutions to improve Black faculty satisfaction. This diversity plan has to include all of the institution's constituents and it needs to be ongoing and encompass classroom dynamics and practices. Furthermore, it must start at the highest echelons of leadership. In a related comment, a woman who had taught at a public midwestern university for nearly six years said "Sensitivity training is needed. There must be support for it from university administration, beginning with the president. There must be a concerted effort for the university to commit to diversity." A professor in the Pacific Northwest said, "There should be ongoing diversity training for all staff, faculty, and administration." A man who taught at a private research university in the Northeast said, "Ethnic and pluralistic training of faculty, staff, and students is necessary in order to increase Black faculty satisfaction."

Some faculty also spoke about what the diversity training should actually entail. For example, a woman at a community college in the Midwest said the diversity training should include "increased dialogue about race and its effects on job satisfaction." Moreover, some participants emphasized that the training should underscore the fact that faculty who incorporate multiculturalism and diversity issues into the curriculum should not be penalized when students are resistant. To illustrate this point, a woman who had taught at a public research university in the West for less than three years stated, "Don't take students' evaluations so seriously, especially when one is teaching diversity-required courses." A woman at a southwestern public research university made a similar recommendation: "Stand with and support faculty when students and other faculty complain about Black faculty," she said.

A recurring theme among the recommendations was that diversity training should produce specific results leading to an increase in Black faculty satisfaction. According to another questionnaire respondent, these results should include "increased sensitivity, equality in treatment, and fairness." Another professor, a woman who had taught in the South for nearly ten years, made a similar remark. She stated that Black faculty satisfaction will increase when institutions become "consistently fair in their treatment of everyone."

Support

Another frequently cited recommendation pertained to support for Black faculty. Forty-three percent of the questionnaire respondents who wrote recommendations made comments that underscored the link between increasing Black faculty satisfaction and providing adequate support. Numerous respondents equated support with mentoring. For example, a male professor who had taught at his current institution for nearly six years said that in order to increase Black faculty satisfaction institutions must "provide necessary mentoring and support." A woman in the Southwest said that in addition to "encouraging mentorship, universities should discourage working to be liked or appreciated." A woman who taught in the Northwest said that mentoring programs should be "formal," instead of informal and haphazard.

Whereas many of the respondents wrote about the need for mentoring in general, several emphasized that mentoring is a major factor in retaining junior faculty and in increasing their job satisfaction. For example, a woman who taught in the South said that although faculty development programs are needed to increase Black faculty satisfaction, "mentoring junior faculty" is a must. A male in the Northwest made a similar remark. He stated, "There needs to be deliberate, systematic support for Black faculty by the institution, and the institution should designate mentors for new faculty." A professor who had taught in the Southeast for less than three years urged postsecondary institutions to "provide a mentor-mentee forum for new faculty."

In addition to providing individual support for Black faculty in the form of mentors, several participants in the study spoke about the need for group support for Black faculty. This support, they said, should come from within the institution as well as outside of the institution. A woman who had taught at an institution in the Southeast for less than three years said, "Provide organizations and outside groups as support" for Black faculty. A woman who taught at a community college in the West said that "group support and group encouragement" are needed. A woman who taught in the Southeast said that technology could be used to provide more support for Black faculty and urged leaders in higher education to "Develop a web-based community, so there is support regardless of where you are located."

In addition to the need for mentorship and group support, several faculty made suggestions about other types of support that could increase Black faculty satisfaction. A male professor in the Midwest suggested that institutions conduct a "needs assessment, implement suggestions, and make sure that Black faculty get actively involved." A woman who had taught at an HBCU for less than three years was less specific. She said that institutions can increase Black faculty satisfaction by "making the environment conducive to growth." A female professor in the Midwest said that increasing Black faculty satisfaction entails "listening to their concerns and working to problem solve." Several respondents spoke about the importance of making Black faculty feel valued. For instance, a woman who had taught at a community college in the Southwest for more than ten years said, "Value their opinions, incorporate their ideas, and validate Black faculty." Finally, a professor at a research university in the Midwest said increasing Black faculty satisfaction requires "recognition, support, and full information" for them.

Professional Duties

Nearly one-fifth of the questionnaire respondents who wrote suggestions about how the Academy can increase Black faculty satisfaction focused on issues pertaining to the professional responsibilities of the professoriate. These issues included teaching, conducting research, and serving on committees. Comments about teaching tended to target the teaching load. For example, a male who had taught at a public research university in the Southwest for less than one year said simply, "Lower the teaching load." A woman who had taught at a private university for many years said that institutions should "Provide a balance between the teaching load and research responsibilities."

In addition to the need for a lighter teaching load and more time for research, as several faculty suggested, other respondents spoke about the need for institutions to assist Black faculty in other ways with their research agenda. A male who had taught at a northeastern public four-year comprehensive university for nearly nine years said that increasing Black faculty satisfaction requires "support with writing journal articles." A woman who taught at an HBCU said, "Provide opportunities in support of Black faculty's research." A male who taught in the Northeast said institutions should "place more value on the interests of Black faculty." Without going into detail about specific types of support to assist Black faculty with their research, several respondents simply wrote, "support for research is needed." However, a few specified that "networking" and a "supportive network for research" are important factors in increasing Black faculty satisfaction.

Another series of comments focused on the need to reduce the committee workload. One respondent, a professor in the Southwest, said that "non-relevant committee work should be eradicated." A professor who had taught in the Northeast for less than three years, said there should be "less demand for committee service." A professor who had taught at a public research university in the West for less than three years said she was experiencing "burn out from being on ALL [emphasis hers] committees." A professor in the Southeast said that not only should the committee workload be decreased, but more professional development resources are needed to increase Black faculty satisfaction.

Compensation and Other Incentives

Ten percent of the respondents who made recommendations said that increasing Black faculty satisfaction requires better compensation and other incentives. Although some faculty were not specific and merely said, "Provide necessary incentives," some were more specific. For example, a professor who had taught at a southeastern, private, four-year university for many years made four recommendations: "More sabbatical leaves, higher salaries, smaller classes, and more resources." A professor who had taught at an HBCU for nearly nine years said that in addition to "respect," increasing Black faculty satisfaction requires "better monetary benefits and more flex time." A professor at a southwestern public research university had only one recommendation: "money," he wrote. Another said, "competitive salary packages" are needed for Black faculty. A male professor in the Northeast said that postsecondary institutions should offer "market pay scale" to faculty in order to increase Black faculty satisfaction.

Other Recommendations

Eight percent of the respondents who made suggestions gave "other" recommendations. In general, these suggestions pertained to tenure, promotion, and the unwritten rules of the Academy. A recurring message was that increasing Black faculty satisfaction requires fairer tenure and promotion practices. For example, a female who had taught in the Northeast for less than three years said postsecondary institutions should "Promote more scholars of color." The need for honest dialogue, respect for the work of Black faculty, a broader definition of "good" teaching, and respect for community service and respect for mentoring African American students were additional recommendations that faculty made.

Summary: "Outing" the "Culture of Arrogance" in the Academy

In October 2004, one of us, Thompson, gave a presentation at the University of South Florida in Tampa. The main title of her presentation, "A Mighty Long and Tedious Journey: Changing Educators' Perceptions of African American Students and Parents"(Thompson, 2004a), came from a song that she used to sing as a child in a church choir. The gist of the song was "the road to a better life is very difficult." Since those childhood days as a choir member, this author has concluded that changing the mind-set of many K-postsecondary educators about African Americans is equally as challenging as navigating the road to a better life. This mind-set that is based on negative beliefs that equate African Americans and black culture with pathology and inferiority is rooted in racism and deficit theories. In this author's opinion, one result is that this mind-set has created a "culture of arrogance" in American society, especially among educators. This "culture of arrogance" is characterized by four beliefs, in this author's opinion: (1) Whites are smarter than Blacks, (2) Blacks do not have the aptitude to do outstanding work, (3) Whites know what is best for Black students, and (4) the research of Black scholars is inferior to the work of Whites (Thompson, 2004a). In fact, this last belief was borne out in the current study, and in the work of other researchers. In our study, for example, we found that a substantial percentage of the participants said that at their institution, African American faculty are less respected than other faculty, and the research of African Americans who specialize in black issues is less respected than other research. Other researchers have reached the same conclusion (Gregory, 1995; Hilliard, 2002; Turner & Myers, 2000; Watkins, 2002; White & Siwatu, 2002). Even more telling is the fact that one-third of the participants in our study said that at their institution, their knowledge about their race and culture was not respected by their colleagues, department chair, or dean. Another example is that one of our White graduate students has repeatedly told one of us that her colleagues in the Reading Department at a large, state university in Los Angeles have made similar comments whenever the student cites the work of Black researchers. In fact, according to this student, they have even refused to read the work of Black researchers and insist that Black researchers "don't know what they're talking about," even when the topic in question is "How to teach Black children to read."

A recurring message that has emerged throughout this book is that many factors are linked to Black faculty satisfaction or dissatisfaction at their current institution. One of those factors is the need to feel valued and respected at work. This means that the research, contributions, experiences, and knowledge of Black faculty must be given as much weight as that of their non-Black colleagues. However, in institutions where the "culture of arrogance" prevails, this is unlikely to occur.

Like our peers who have done similar work (Bell, 1994; Gregory, 1995; Jones, 2002; Mabokela & Green, 2001; Moses, 1989; Turner & Meyers, 2000; and others), in this chapter, we have given faculty and administrators in the Academy another opportunity to hear the voices of Black faculty regarding the ways in which higher education can become more inclusive and, thereby, more effective. Many participants in our study said that mentoring students of color is one of the most rewarding aspects of their jobs. Through mentoring, they are able to prepare Black students for life in the Academy. They are also "giving back to the Black community" via mentoring, as well as ensuring that the pipeline of prospective professors of color will not dry up.

The results that we presented in this chapter also revealed that contrary to popular opinion in the Academy, conducting research is not only important to Black faculty (Antonio, 2002; W. Watkins, 2002; White & Siwatu, 2002), but it is also one of the most rewarding aspects of their job. Furthermore, as other researchers have concluded, performing community service continues to be important to Black faculty (Jarmon, 2001; White & Siwatu, 2002), and, often, Black faculty's community service work is closely tied to their research agenda in the form of attempting to improve social conditions. This finding has a long tradition among Black academics. For example, DuBois, who has been labeled as "the most important Black leader of the twentieth century and the spiritual father of the contemporary civil rights movement" (Robbins, 1996, p. 26), conducted a seminal study that resulted in the book *The Philadelphia Negro*, which was published in the late 1800s. Twenty years later, Charles S. Johnson, a social scientist who became the first Black president of Fisk University, conducted a study on the Chicago race riots, which was published as several chapters in *The Negro in Chicago*. According to Robbins, "Both studies were innovative in making use of survey techniques and demographic data; both were grounded in the then optimistic social science conviction that research could lead to reform" (1996, p. 26). Like many African American researchers today, both Johnson and DuBois received their share of criticism and disrespect. Nevertheless, they produced bodies of work that made important contributions to social science research. In DuBois' case, that includes *Black Reconstruction* and *The Souls of Black Folks*. Johnson's work includes *Shadow of the Plantation* and *Growing Up in the Black Belt*.

Today, in postsecondary institutions throughout the United States countless Black faculty continue to follow in the steps of these and other renowned researchers; however, the "culture of arrogance" that permeates many institutions continues to cause their work to receive less respect and attention than it deserves. In order to improve the situation, and other problems that contribute to Black faculty dissatisfaction and attrition, leaders in the Academy must be willing to make specific changes. The first of course, is destroying the "culture of arrogance" (Thompson, 2004a) that prevents them from listening to the voices of marginalized groups and taking them seriously. In other words, as Turner and Myers (2000) stated, "We need to credit the knowledge shared by [faculty of color] rather than maintaining the ignorance of privilege and the privilege of ignorance" (p. 112). According to the participants in our study, necessary changes include improving the institutional climate through the aggressive recruitment of Black faculty, Black students, and Black administrators (Hale, 2002; Nelms, 2002); identifying racist and culturally insensitive attitudes and behaviors that lead to dissatisfaction; providing faculty, staff, and students with ongoing diversity training (Hale, 2002); providing adequate support for Black faculty through mentoring (Alfred, 2001; Gregory, 1995; Turner & Myers, 2000; Williams, 2001); valuing their input (Jones, 2001; Turner & Myers, 2000); and ensuring that the teaching load and committee work do not become deterrents to conducting research (Gregory, 1995; White & Siwatu, 2002). In the next chapter, we will say more about the need to eradicate the "culture of arrogance" (Thompson, 2004a) in order for progress to occur in the Academy, and we issue a call for courageous leaders—at all levels of the Academy—to step up to the plate.

8

CONCLUSION: CALLING ALL COURAGEOUS LEADERS!

A BOUT FIVE YEARS AGO, one of the authors of this book applied for a mini grant at the public PWI where she worked as an assistant professor. At this institution, university officials strongly encouraged junior faculty to apply for the annual grants, in an effort to help faculty facilitate their research goals. The author was excited to learn this, because at the time, she was in the early stages of a project that entailed collecting data from African American high school seniors. So, she submitted a proposal to the committee of professors who would determine which applicants would receive funding and which would not.

When the committee sent her their written feedback, she was happy to learn that although they recommended that she address a few minor points, most of the feedback about her proposal was positive. More important, the committee had agreed to approve her for a mini grant. However, one of the written comments from a full professor troubled her. This elderly White male had cautioned, "Be careful. You're a Black person who plans to talk to Black kids in order to find out negative things about the school system." Evidently, he was warning the author to be honest. Perhaps he believed that Black professors who conduct research using Black samples are likely to resort to dishonesty, so warnings are necessary. In other words, he may have been validating Turner and Myers's assertion that not only are the voices of faculty of color ". . . largely ignored [but] what they have to say is deemed inherently unreliable" (2000, p. 111). Obviously, he was also exposing the unwritten rule of the Academy pertaining to less respect being given to Black faculty who study "black topics," a rule that we discussed in chapter 4 and that other researchers have written about (Akbar, 2002; Hilliard, 2002; Jarmon, 2001; Turner & Myers, 2000; White & Siwatu, 2002). Moreover, he apparently assumed that the author had a hidden agenda—to find negativity—even though the proposal had explicitly stated that she wanted to get a comprehensive look at students' K-12 schooling experiences.

In addition to exposing an unwritten rule of the Academy, the senior professor's warning illustrated one way in which the "culture of arrogance" that permeates U.S. society and the K-postsecondary education system can manifest itself. As we stated in the previous chapter, this "culture of arrogance" is characterized by four beliefs: (1) Whites are smarter than Blacks, (2) Blacks do not have the aptitude to do outstanding work, (3) Whites know what is best for Black students, and (4) the research of Black scholars is inferior to the work of Whites (Thompson, 2004a).

We ended the previous chapter and began this chapter of the book with details about the "culture of arrogance" that permeates American society, but especially the Academy, because as African American researchers, we suspect that this pervasive problem will cause some of the members of postsecondary institutions who are in the best positions to change the status quo to discount our work. Instead of examining the main messages that surfaced and giving careful consideration to our suggestions and the recommendations of the study's participants, they will quibble—as academics are notorious for doing—over the very limitations that we spoke candidly about in the introduction of this book. "They used a non-random sample, and their sample size is too small!" our critics will proclaim. "Therefore, their study is not important, representative, or generalizable." What they will probably not state publicly, but will undoubtedly think is, "They're angry Black women, so we don't have to listen to them anyway." After all, many Whites have historically portrayed Black women as being angry and aggressive as an excuse to ignore their views and voices. Then, they will go about their business, perhaps subconsciously, but definitely arrogantly, of engaging in some of the same practices, such as devaluing the scholarship of Black researchers, that have created the inhospitable climate in many postsecondary institutions that we described in previous chapters.

Jones (2002) expressed similar sentiments about his edited book, *Making It on Broken Promises: African American Male Scholars Confront the Culture of Higher Education*, when he wrote, "I am positive that there will be some in the Academy who will . . . reject the opportunity to think critically about what is postulated in this book. This blatant disregard for critically dealing with inequality in the Academy is at the base of why this book was developed" (p. xiii). Turner and Myers (2000) described the Academy well when they wrote, "For some, efforts to transform the culture of higher education will be embraced as a long overdue renaissance. Others who have invested much of their lives to building the institution as it now exists will experience change as a kind of death or great loss" (p. 220).

In spite of the Academy's long history of resisting change (Akbar, 2002; Hilliard, 2002; Jones, 2002; Smith, 1995; Turner & Myers, 2000; W. Watkins, 2002; White & Siwatu, 2002) and full inclusiveness, we hope that unlike the individuals who uphold and practice the behaviors that are characteristic of the "culture of arrogance" (Thompson, 2004a), others will, at the very least, look at the recurring themes and recommendations in this book with an open mind. Moreover, we hope that some readers will even be receptive, if not enthusiastic, about using this information as a springboard for improving higher education, so that unlike the young African American professor whom we described in the previous chapter who decided to leave the Academy completely, other Black professors will find the workplace so supportive that they will choose to remain. In other words, as Turner and Myers (2000) said, we hope that "Many in the academic community will welcome the opportunity for self-examination and energetic dialogue that must accompany institutional change" (p.

220). A final story illustrates what can happen when postsecondary institutions attain the "ideal."

In October 2004, as we neared the completion of this book, one of us attended the Laser Research Writing and Collaboration Think Tank at the University of South Florida in Tampa, as we mentioned in the previous chapter. One of the participants at the think tank, an African American woman, shared a heartwarming story with this author that is pertinent to the study that we conducted for this book. This professor had taught at a large, four-year comprehensive PWI in California for nearly thirty-five years. At the time when she was hired in the 1960s, she was the first African American her speech pathology department had ever hired. "When I went there, I only planned to stay for one year," she said. However, she ended up not only staying for more than three decades, but at the time when she shared her story with the author, she appeared to be very content at her institution. All of the reasons that she shared have surfaced throughout this book as issues that have an impact on Black faculty satisfaction or dissatisfaction. When asked to provide specific examples of why she had remained at her institution for so long, the senior professor explained, "I found a university that let me be creative and I've done things that I enjoy. For example, I wanted to do international work, and the university didn't stop me. I went to Saudi Arabia and taught for two years. I also did some satellite programs, and we've done programs in Guam."

In addition to permitting her to pursue her passions, administrators also allowed this professor to recruit more students of color. She stated:

> I also was allowed to recruit minority students. I created a program, and we recruited and graduated more minority students in speech pathology [than any other speech pathology department] in the state of California. . . . Speech pathology is predominantly women and predominantly White. . . . [But] we've graduated more African American students, more Spanish-speaking students, you name it.

One of the first things that I did as a new assistant professor was [I] advocated for the abolition of the GRE as a requirement. So, we got rid of it in 1970. . . . The fact that we graduated them and they've passed the national exam [indicates] that we have an excellent program. Getting rid of the GRE didn't lower standards; it got rid of discrimination that was inherent in the test.

Another factor that contributed to this professor's contentment at her university was the fact that she believed that her colleagues and administrators viewed her as a valuable member of the faculty. She remarked, "They allow a certain level of autonomy among the faculty, but also, there was a level of appreciation of the kind of work that minority faculty do, in terms of cultural information, Afrocentric research, and publications. I'm sure that at some universities, they have no respect for Afrocentric research and publications. . . . But my university accepted that, and continues to."

The last factor that caused this professor to remain satisfied enough to stay at the same institution for more than three decades was the mentoring that she received. She stated, "The chair of my department at that time [when she was hired], recruited me and mentored me. She is a White woman who is now almost 80 years old, and she continues to mentor me."

The nearly thirty-five years that this African American speech pathologist has spent at one institution have not been easy. From the late 1960s to 2000, she was not only the sole African American in her department, but the only person of color as well. At the time when she and one of the authors of this book met, she remained the only faculty member of color in her department, because the other faculty member of color who was later hired died in 2004. Nevertheless, she has been satisfied enough to remain at the university and during much of that time she has been influential in the decision-making process and has even served as program director and department chair for many years.

We wanted to conclude this book with her inspirational story, because it demonstrates that PWIs can indeed successfully recruit and retain Black faculty when all of the factors that constitute a supportive work environment, such as mentoring, respect for the scholarship, knowledge, background experiences, culture, and contributions of Black faculty, as well as fair tenure and promotion practices and full inclusion in the decision-making process are present. Her story also underscores the recurring theme in this book that "Leadership makes the difference" (Brown, 1995; Hale, 2002; Lipman-Blumen, 2005, 1998; Nelms, 2002; Smith, 1995; Thompson, 2003). Moreover, we suspect that the participants in our study who were very satisfied at their current institution had good leaders at the helm of their institution, or at least as their immediate supervisor.

In *The Art of Leadership: A Practical Guide for People in Positions of Responsibility*, Walters (1987) described the characteristics of effective leaders. He stated, "Genuine leadership is of only one type: supportive. It leads people. It does not drive them" (p. 11). In *The Allure of Toxic Leaders*, Lipman-Blumen (2005) identified the characteristics of bad leaders and the effects of their destructive leadership practices on organizations. She maintained that toxic leaders are often cowards who "shrink from the difficult choices" (p. 22) that need to be made. In our opinion, in the Academy, sometimes, this cowardice comes from leaders' fear of angering a resistant faculty and others who oppose full inclusiveness. However, according to Hale (2002), "There is absolutely no substitute for strong leadership that will make the point that systemic change is an institutional imperative. . . . Goals for faculty diversity are best realized when leaders are not afraid to make it clear that diversity is high on their agenda and that they will not be intimidated by the naysayers" (p. 164). In other cases, leaders behave in toxic or cowardly ways because they genuinely do not know what to do (Smith, 1995). Lipman-Blumen (2005) said that toxic leaders fail "both to understand the nature of relevant problems and to act competently and effectively in leadership situations" (p. 22).

One of the reasons why we wrote this book is that both of us have worked under toxic leaders at one point or another during our careers as professors. In some cases, we became dissatisfied enough to leave those institutions. We have learned from our own experiences, from research, and the participants in our study that academic leaders—administrators at all levels—can become impediments to Black faculty retention, or they can provide Black faculty with the much-needed support that can have a positive effect on their attitudes about the Academy and their sense of well-being at their institution. The quantitative and qualitative data and the related literature that we presented throughout this book underscore the important role that leaders play in increasing or decreasing Black faculty satisfaction and dissatisfaction in postsecondary institutions. Our study clearly shows that those in leadership roles are included among the factors that contribute to whether Black faculty decide to leave or remain at an institution. When leadership is not supportive, allows a racist climate to exist, ignores the complaints of Black faculty, does not handle racist situations well, or does not value the community service, voices, and research of Black faculty, dissatisfaction is a likely outcome, because these disparaging attitudes and behaviors will permeate the institutional climate, and others will engage in the same behaviors.

There is no excuse for any leader in the Academy to be ineffective, for a plethora of research exists that contains the blueprint for successful leadership (Hale, 2002; Hrabowski, 1999, 2001; Lindsey et al., 1999; Lipman-Blumen, 2005, 1998; Louque, 2002; Nelms, 2002; Smith, 1995; Turner & Myers, 2000; Walters, 1987; and others) and details about how organizations can be transformed by good leadership. Recurring themes underscore the fact that effective leaders are courageous in implementing change, they promote full inclusiveness, they respect dissenting voices, they do not pit one group against the other, they are proactive, they are assertive, they make their constituents feel valued, and they create a supportive work environment. Moreover, as the participants in our study repeatedly said, they must ensure that a critical mass of members of underrepresented groups are hired and become integral parts of the organization, and they must provide ongoing diversity training for all constituents.

Hence, to us, the dilemma of increasing Black faculty satisfaction and, thereby, retention rates, has an obvious but not simple solution. The institutional climate must change at the most fundamental levels. As the data that we have presented throughout this book suggest, improving the climate of institutions in ways that are likely to increase Black faculty satisfaction and retention rates must encompass all sectors of the institutional community and result in a positive effect on students, staff, faculty, and administrators, and a dismantling of the "culture of arrogance" that permeates the Academy (Thompson, 2004a). Ideally, it should begin with visionary and courageous leaders. So, we conclude this book by issuing a call for courageous leaders among faculty, department chairs, deans, and other administrators who truly desire to see the Academy reach its maximum potential to step up to the plate. As Turner and Myers (2000) said, "A high level of commitment by people throughout the institution is essential. . . . To achieve the goal of faculty diversity, everyone has a role to play in transforming the academic workplace environment into one that affirms and nurtures all of its members" (p. 176). Therefore, we end this book with a call for all courageous leaders in the Academy to rise to the challenge of making higher education fully inclusive, and with a reminder that "the essence of leadership is action" (Walters, 1987, p. 104). Effective leaders "adapt [their] actions to reality" (p. 99). We believe that the realities of life in the Academy for the Black faculty that we studied and their recommendations, speak for themselves about what leaders must do in order to increase Black faculty satisfaction. First, and foremost, this much-needed action plan must begin with courage.

REFERENCES

Aguirre, A., Jr., Martinez, R., & Hernandez, A. (1993). Majority and minority faculty perceptions in academe. *Research in Higher Education, 34*(3), 371–385.

Akbar, N. (2002). The psychological dilemma of African American academicians. In L. Jones (Ed.), *Making it on broken promises: African American male scholars confront the culture of higher education* (pp. 31–41). Sterling, VA: Stylus.

Alfred, M. V. (2001). Success in the ivory tower: Lessons from Black tenured female faculty at a major research university. In R. O. Mabokela & A. L. Green (Eds.), *Sisters of the Academy: Emergent Black women scholars in higher education* (pp. 57–79). Sterling, VA: Stylus.

American Association of University Women. (1991). *Shortchanging girls, shortchanging America: Executive summary.* Washington, DC: American Association of University Women.

American Institute of Stress. (2005). Job Stress. Retrieved February 15, 2005, from www.stress.org.

Anderson, W., Jr., Frierson, H., & Lewis, T. (1979). Black survival in White America. *Journal of Negro Education, 48*(1), 92–102.

Antonio, A. (2002). Faculty of color reconsidered: Reassessing contributions to scholarship. *The Journal of Higher Education, 73*(5), 582–602.

Association of American Law Schools (1996, April). Retaining faculty of color. Newsletter. Retrieved July 8, 2003, from http://www.aals.org.ml-t3.html.

Astin, H. S., Antonio, A. L., Cress, C. M., & Astin, A. W. (1997). *Race and ethnicity in the American professoriate, 1995–1996.* Los Angeles: Higher Education Research Institutes, Graduate School of Education and Information Studies.

Au, K. (1993). *Literacy instruction in multicultural settings.* Orlando: Harcourt Brace.

Baez, B., & Centra, J. A. (1995). *Tenure, promotion, and reappointment: Legal and administrative implications.* East Lansing, MI: ERIC Clearinghouse on Higher Education, the George Washington University in cooperation with ASHE, Association for the Study of Higher Education.Washington, DC: Graduate School of Education and Development, the George Washington University.

Bell, D. (1994). *Confronting authority: Reflections of an ardent protester.* Boston: Beacon.

Benjamin, L. (1997). *Black women in the Academy: Promises and perils.* Gainesville: University Press of Florida.

Blackwell, J. E. (1983). *Networking and mentoring: A study of cross-generational experiences of Black professionals.* Bayside, NY: General Hall.

Boice, R. (1993). New faculty involvement for women and minorities. *Research in Higher Education, 34*(3), 291–341.

Bonner, F. (2004). Black professors: On the track but out of the loop. *Chronicle of Higher Education.* Retrieved June 11, 2004, from http://chronicle.com/weekly/v50/i40/40b01101.htm.

Bowser, B., Auletta, G., & Jones, T. (1999). *Confronting diversity issues on campus.* Newbury, CA: Sage.

Brown, M., Davis, G., & McClendon, S. (1999). Mentoring graduate students of color: Myths, models, and modes. *Peabody Journal of Education, 74*(2), 105–18.

Brown, S. V. (1988). *Increasing minority faculty: An elusive goal.* Princeton, NJ: Graduate Records Board and Educational Testing Service.

Brown, T. (1995). *Black lies, white lies: The truth according to Tony Brown.* New York: William Morrow.

Bugeja, M. J. (2002, July 20). Is congeniality overrated? *Chronicle of Higher Education.* Career Network. Retrieved February 20, 2003, from www.chronicle.com/jobs/2002/07/2002073001c.htm.

Carter, D. J., & O'Brien, E. O. (1993). Employment and hiring patterns for faculty of color. *American Council on Education Research Briefs, 4*(6), 1–16.

Childs, F., & Palmer, N. (1999). *Going off: A guide for Black women who've just about had enough.* New York: St. Martin's.

Cloke, K., & Goldsmith, J. (2000). *Resolving conflicts at work: A complete guide for everyone on the job.* San Francisco: Jossey-Bass.

Comer, J. P. (2002). My view. In S. Denbo & L. Beaulieu (Eds.), *Improving schools for African American students* (pp. 5–11). Springfield, IL: Charles C. Thomas.

Daniels, C. (2004, July 20). Getty apologizes for docent-related incident. *Los Angeles Times*, p. B4.

Davie, M. R. (1949). *Negroes in American society.* New York: McGraw-Hill.

Dortch, T., Jr. (2000). *The miracles of mentoring: The joy of investing in our future.* New York: Doubleday.

Drew, D. E. (1996). *Aptitude revisited: Rethinking math and science education for America's next century.* Baltimore, MD: Johns Hopkins University Press.

Duberman, M. B. (1989). *Paul Robeson.* New York: Ballantine.

Ellis, C. M. (2002). Examining the pitfalls facing African American males. In L. Jones (Ed.), *Making it on broken promises: African American male scholars confront the culture of higher education* (pp. 61–71). Sterling, VA: Stylus.

Ferguson, A. A. (2001). *Bad boys: Public schools in the making of black masculinity.* Ann Arbor: University of Michigan Press.

Fleming, J. E. (1976). *The lengthening shadow of slavery.* Washington, DC: Howard University Press.

Fogg, P. (2004a, June 18). Hello . . . I must be going: Most assistant professors at top Ivy League universities won't be sticking around for the long term. *Chronicle of Higher Education*, A10–12.

Fogg, P. (2004b, June 25). AAUP censures a college, criticizes another, and drops 3 from list. *Chronicle of Higher Education*, A21.

Fordham, S. (1996). *Blacked out: Dilemmas of race, identity, and success at Capital High.* Chicago: University of Chicago Press.

Galbraith, J. K. (1990). *A tenured professor.* New York: Houghton Mifflin.

Garcia, M. (Ed.). (2000). *Succeeding in an academic career: A guide for faculty of color.* Westport, CT: Greenwood.

Green, P. (2000). African American men and the Academy. In L. Jones (Ed.), *Brothers of the Academy: Up and coming Black scholars earning our way in higher education* (pp. 3–20). Sterling, VA: Stylus.

Gregory, S. T. (1995). *Black women in the Academy: The secrets to success and achievement.* New York: University Press of America.

Hale, F. W., Jr. (2002). Visualizing the framework for access and success: Democracy demands that we care. In L. Jones (Ed.), *Making it on broken promises: African American male scholars confront the culture of higher education* (pp. 161–170). Sterling, VA: Stylus.

Hale-Benson, J. E. (1986). *Black Children: Their roots, culture, and learning styles*. Baltimore, MD: Johns Hopkins University Press.

Haynes-Burton, S. (2004). *Application of organizational leadership: Establishing a formal mentoring program*. Unpublished doctoral dissertation, Pepperdine University, Malibu, CA.

Hilliard, A. G., III (2002). One by one, or one: Africans and the Academy. In L. Jones (Ed.), *Making it on broken promises: African American male scholars confront the culture of higher education* (pp. 43–59). Sterling, VA: Stylus.

hooks, b. (2003). *Rock my soul: Black people and self-esteem*. New York: Atria.

Hrabowski, F. A., III. (1999, December). Embracing excellence and diversity. *The School Administrator* [Electronic version]. Retrieved November 18, 2004, from www.aasa.org/publications/sa/1999_12/hrabowski.htm.

Hrabowski, F. A., III. (2001). The Meyerhoff Scholars Program: Producing high-achieving minority students in mathematics and science. *Notices of the AMS, 48*(1), 26–28.

Hrabowski, F. A., III, Maton, K. I., Greene, M. L., & Greif, G. L. (2002). *Overcoming the odds: Raising academically successful African American young women*. New York: Oxford University Press.

Hrabowski, F. A., III, Maton, K. I., & Greif, G. L. (1998). *Beating the odds: Raising academically successful African American males*. New York: Oxford University Press.

Ingersoll, R. M. (1999). The problem of underqualified teachers in American secondary schools. *Educational Researcher, 28*(2), 26–37.

Irvine, J. J. (1992). Making teacher education culturally responsive. In M. Dilworth (Ed.), *Diversity in teacher education* (pp. 79–92). Washington, DC: American Association of Colleges for Teacher Education.

Jackson, J. (2004). The story is not in the numbers: Academic socialization and diversifying the faculty. *National Women's Studies Association Journal, 16*(1), 172–185.

Jarmon, B. (2001). Unwritten rules of the game. In R. O. Mabokela & A. L. Green (Eds.), *Sisters of the Academy: Emergent Black women scholars in higher education* (pp. 175–181). Sterling, VA: Stylus.

Jasper, J. M. (2001, August 31). Institutions are not your friends. *Chronicle of*

Higher Education. Career Network. Retrieved February 20, 2003, from http://chronicle.com/jobs/2001/08/2001083102c.htm.

Jayate, S. E. (2002). Racism on the tenure track. *Chronicle of Higher Education.* Career Network. Retrieved February 20, 2003, from http://chronicle.com/jobs/2002/11/2002112601c.htm.

Johnson, B., & Harvey, W. (2002). The socialization of Black college faculty: Implications for policy and practice. *Review of Higher Education,* *25*(3), 297–314.

Jones, L. (Ed.). (2001). *Retaining African Americans in higher education.* Sterling, VA: Stylus.

Jones, L. (Ed.). (2002). *Making it on broken promises: African American male scholars confront the culture of higher education.* Sterling, VA: Stylus.

Kaplan, C. (2002). *Zora Neale Hurston: A life in letters.* New York: Doubleday.

Ladson-Billings, G. (1996). Silences as weapons: Challenges of a Black professor teaching white students. *Theory into Practice, 35*(2), 79–85.

Ladson-Billings, G. (2001). *Crossing over to Canaan: The journey of new teachers in diverse classrooms.* San Francisco: Jossey-Bass.

Levine, A. (1993). *Higher learning in America: 1980–2000.* Baltimore, MD: Johns Hopkins University Press.

Lewis, D. L. (1993). *W. E. B. DuBois: Biography of a race, 1868–1919.* New York: Henry Holt.

Lindsey, R. B., Nuri Robins, K., & Terrell, R. D. (1999). *Cultural proficiency: A manual for school leaders.* Thousand Oaks, CA: Corwin Press.

Lipman-Blumen, J. (1998, January/February). Connective leadership: What business needs to learn from academe. *Change,* 49–53.

Lipman-Blumen, J. (2005). *The allure of toxic leaders: Why we follow destructive bosses and corrupt politicians—and how we can survive them.* New York: Oxford University Press.

Louque, A. (1994). *The participation of minorities in higher education.* Unpublished doctoral dissertation, Pepperdine University, Malibu, CA.

Louque, A. (1999). Factors influencing academic attainment for African American women PhD recipients: An ethnographic study of their persistence. *Negro Educational Review, 51*(3–4), 101–108.

Louque, A. (2002). Spicing it up: Blending perspectives of leadership and cultural values from Hispanic American and African American women scholars. *Educational Leadership Review, 3*(2), 28–31.

Mabokela, R. O., & Green, A. (Eds.). (2001). *Sisters of the Academy: Emergent Black women scholars in higher education.* Sterling, VA: Stylus.

Mickelson, R. A., & Oliver, M. L. (1991). Making the short list: Black candidates and the faculty recruitment process. In P. G. Altbach & K. Lomotey (Eds.), *The racial crisis in American higher education.* New York: State University of New York Press.

Moore, W., Jr., & Wagstaff, L. H. (1974). *Black educators in White colleges.* San Francisco: Jossey-Bass.

Moses, Y. T. (1989). *Black women in academe: Issues and strategies. Project on the status and education of women.* Washington, DC: Association of American Colleges.

National Center for Education Statistics. (2003). *Staff in postsecondary institutions, Fall 2001, and salaries of full-time instructional faculty, 2001–02.* Washington, DC: U.S. Department of Education.

National Education Association. (2002). Faculty satisfaction. *Update, 8*(2). Washington, DC: NEA Higher Education Research Center.

National Institute for Occupational Safety and Health. (2005). Stress. Retreived February 15, 2005, from www.cdc.gov/niash/stresswk.html.

Nelms, C. (2002). The prerequisites for academic leadership. In L. Jones (Ed.), *Making it on broken promises: African American male scholars confront the culture of higher education* (pp. 189–193). Sterling, VA: Stylus.

Nettles, M. T. (1990, August). Success in doctoral programs: Experiences of minority and White students. *American Journal of Education, 98*(4), 494–522.

Oakes, J., & Rogers, J. (2002, October 8). Diploma penalty misplaces blame. *Los Angeles Times,* p. M2.

Olsen, D., Maple, S. A., & Stage, F. K. (1995). Women and minority faculty job satisfaction. *Journal of Higher Education, 66*(3), 267–291.

Olsen, L. (1997). *Made in America: Immigrant students in our public schools.* New York: The New Press.

Ostrow, E. (2002). Don't go it alone. *Chronicle of Higher Education.* Career Network. Retrieved February 20, 2003, from http://chronicle.com/jobs/2002/08/2002081201c.htm.

Perna, L. W. (2002). Retaining African Americans in higher education: Challenging paradigms for retaining students, faculty and administrators. *Journal of Higher Education, 73*(5), 652–659.

Perry, T. (2003). Competing theories of group achievement. In T. Perry, C. Steele, & A. Hilliard III (Eds.), *Young, gifted and Black: Promoting high achievement among African-American students* (pp. 52–86). Boston: Beacon.

Phillip, M. (1995). Anyplace but here: UIC professor's resignation raises questions of tolerance and acceptance. *Black Issues in Higher Education*, *12*(6), 18.

Quezada, R., & Louque, A. (2004). The absence of diversity in the academy: Faculty of color in educational administration programs. *Education*, *125*(2), 213–221.

Rankin, C. (2002). Equity and excellence: Is there room for African American Ph.D.s? In Jones (Ed.), *Making it on broken promises: African American male scholars confront the culture of higher education* (pp. 73–77). Sterling, VA: Stylus.

Ravitch, D. (1983). *The troubled crusade: American education 1945–1980*. New York: Basic.

Roach, R. (2003). Harvard's new chapter in Black Studies: A neglected African Studies program finally gets a departmental home. *Black Issues in Higher Education*, *20*(17), 26–31.

Robbins, R. (1996). *Sidelines activist: Charles S. Johnson and the struggle for civil rights*. Jackson: University Press of Mississippi.

Rowley, L. (2000). African American men in higher education. In L. Jones (Ed.), *Brothers of the Academy: Up and coming Black scholars earning our way in higher education* (pp. 83–99). Sterling, VA: Stylus.

Sanford, J. (2002, October). Recruiting and retaining faculty of color. *Kiosk*. Retrieved June 11, 2004, from http://www1.umn.edu/urelate/kiosk/1002kiosk/index.html.

Silver, J. H., Dennis, R. W., & Spikes, C. (1988). *Black faculty in traditionally White institutions in selected Adams states: Characteristics, experiences and perceptions*. Statesboro, GA: Southern Education Foundation.

Simmons, R. (2002). *Odd girl out: The hidden culture of aggression in girls*. Orlando, FL: Harcourt Brace.

Smith, D. G. (1995). Organizational implications of diversity in higher education. In M. Chemers, S. Oskamp, & M. A. Costanzo (Eds.), *Diversity in Organizations: New perspectives for a changing workplace*. Thousand Oaks, CA: Sage.

Spann, J. (1990). *Retaining and promoting minority faculty members: Problems and possibilities.* Madison: University of Wisconsin System.

Tack, M. W., & Patitu, C. L. (1992). Faculty job satisfaction: Women and minorities in peril. (ASHE-ERIC Higher Education, Report, No. 4). Washington, DC: George Washington University.

Thomas, C., & Simpson, D. J. (1995). Community, collegiality, and diversity: Is there a conflict of interest in the professoriate? *Journal of Negro Education, 64*(1), 1–5.

Thomas, G. E. (1987). Black students in U.S. graduate and professional schools in the 1980s: A national and institutional assessment. *Harvard Educational Review, 57*(3), 26–279.

Thomas-El, S. (2003). *I choose to stay: A Black teacher refuses to desert the inner city.* New York: Kensington.

Thompson, G. L. (1999). What the numbers really mean: African-American underrepresentation at the doctoral level. *Journal of College Student Retention Research, Theory & Practice, 1*(1), 23–40.

Thompson, G. L. (2002). *African American teens discuss their schooling experiences.* Westport, CT: Greenwood.

Thompson, G. L. (2003). *What African American parents want educators to know.* Westport, CT: Praeger.

Thompson, G. L. (2004a, October 15). *A mighty long and tedious journey: Changing educators' perceptions of African American students and parents.* Paper presented at the Laser Research Writing and Collaboration Think Tank. Tampa: University of South Florida.

Thompson, G. L. (2004b). *Through ebony eyes: What teachers need to know but are afraid to ask about African American students.* San Francisco: Jossey-Bass.

Tierney, W., & Rhoads, R. (1994). *Faculty socialization as cultural process: A mirror of institutional commitment.* Report No. 93–6. ERIC Clearinghouse on Higher Education. George Washington University, in cooperation with ASHE, Association for the Study of Higher Education. Washington, DC: School of Education and Human Development, George Washington University

Toth, E. (2002a). Academic revenge. *Chronicle of Higher Education.* Career Network. Retrieved February 20, 2003, from http://chronicle.com/jobs/2002/01/2002010402c.htm.

Toth, E. (2002b). I thought I mentored her, but . . . *Chronicle of Higher Education*. Career Network. Retrieved February 20, 2003, from http://chronicle.com/jobs/2002/06/2002062401c.htm.

Turner, C. S. V. (2002). Women of color in academe: Living with multiple marginality. *The Journal of Higher Education, 73*(1), 74–93.

Turner, C. S. V., & Myers, S. L., Jr. (2000). *Faculty of color in academe: Bittersweet success*. Needham Heights, MA: Allyn & Bacon.

U.S. Census Bureau. *Statistical abstract of the United States: 2001*. Retrieved March 2, 2002, from http://www.census.gov/hhes/www/img/incpov01/fig08.jpg.

Van Maanen, J., & Schein, E. H. (1979). Toward a theory of organizational socialization. In B. J. Johnson & W. Harvey, *The Socialization of Black College Faculty: Implications for Policy and Practice. Review of Higher Education, 25*(3), 297–314

Walters, J. D. (1987). *The art of leadership: A practical guide for people in positions of responsibility*. New York: MJF Books.

Watkins, S. (Ed). (1944). *Anthology of American Negro literature*. New York: Random House.

Watkins, W. (2002). Understanding the socialization process. In L. Jones (Ed.), *Making it on broken promises: African American male scholars confront the culture of higher education* (pp. 99–105). Sterling, VA: Stylus.

Watts, J. (1995). Identity and the status of Afro-American intellectuals. In M. Berube & C. Nelson (Eds.), *Higher education under fire*. New York: Routledge.

Webster's Universal English Dictionary (2004). Scotland: Geddes & Grosset.

West, C. (2002). Foreword. In L. Jones (Ed.), *Making it on broken promises: African American male scholars confront the culture of higher education* (pp. xi–xii). Sterling, VA: Stylus.

White, J., & Siwatu, K. (2002). Come so far, but so far to go: Interview with Dr. Joseph White. In L. Jones (Ed.), *Making it on broken promises: African American male scholars confront the culture of higher education* (pp. 79–96). Sterling, VA: Stylus.

Williams, L. D. (2001). Coming to terms with being a young, Black female academic in U.S. higher education. In R. O. Mabokela & A. L. Green (Eds.), *Sisters of the Academy: Emergent Black women scholars in higher education* (pp. 93–102). Sterling, VA: Stylus.

Wilson, R. (1988). Developing leadership: Blacks in graduate and profes-
    sional schools. *Journal of Black Studies, 19*(2), 163–173.

Woods, R. L. (2001). Invisible women: The experiences of Black female doc-
    toral students at the University of Michigan. In R. O. Mabokela & A. L.
    Green (Eds.), *Sisters of the Academy: Emergent Black women scholars in
    higher education* (pp. 105–115). Sterling, VA: Stylus.